Love

Through My Sufferings

Jimmy Lee Robinson

authorHOUSE®

AuthorHouse™
1663 Liberty Drive
Bloomington, IN 47403
www.authorhouse.com
Phone: 1-800-839-8640

First published by AuthorHouse   5/4/2010

ISBN: 978-1-4490-7859-1 (e)
ISBN: 978-1-4490-7861-4 (sc)

Library of Congress Control Number: 2010902494

Printed in the United States of America
Bloomington, Indiana

This book is printed on acid-free paper.

Contents

Prayer Is

Prayer Is the Remedy that cures <u>The Great Depression</u>
It might be your only **Opportunity** to make a good impression
Prayer Is the only way to turn our *Nasty* negatives
Into *Productive*, <u>Life Changing</u> **Positives**
Prayer Is the Cornerstone, where the weary rest and the dismayed find **Hope**
Prayer my Brothers and Sisters is the only way we're going to be able to **Cope**
Prayer Is the <u>Correct Answer</u> to every problem in Life
It's what you do when you're looking for a *Good* Husband or a *Good* Wife
Prayer indeed is the **Very Voice of Faith**
Prayer Is something we just can't afford to fake
Prayer Is what reminds us of who **GOD Is** and who we are
Prayer, <u>If Utilized!</u> Will take us very far
Remember, *Prayer* works for *ALL*, <u>no matter What or Who you Are!</u>

Love of GOD

If the **Love of GOD** is in our heart
We'll show it in our lives from the very start
GOD accepts no Love that includes Her and excludes the next man
GODS Love enables the weak and scared man to stand
GODS Love is like no other
SHE Commands me to Love my <u>Sister and Brother</u>
GODS Love is Very Refreshing and Very New
Very Tried and Very True
<u>Unconditional Love</u> is what I'm talking about
GOD Loves You is what I loudly shout
The Creator at this very moment is protecting you
Just doing - doing what She do
The **Love of GOD** don't Cost a Thing
Boom! I've just given you a reason to Sing
GODS Love is going to bring us all together
The **Love of GOD** is what the world needs to make it better
The <u>Love of GOD</u> is about Love
That Rises High Above
From the <u>GOD of Love!</u>

THOU ART

THOU ART the *Most Just of Judges*
Because you're the only one I know who doesn't hold grudges
THOU ART the *Best of Providers*
You're the reason this women standing here NOW is a cancer survivor
THOU ART *My Hope and My Confidence*
Because everything you tell me seems to make sense
THOU ART the *Great* and *Miraculous Lover*
Now that's what I learned from my Dear Mother
THOU ART my *Truest and Best Friend*
Because you're the only one who knows my end
THOU ART my *Only Teacher*
Thanks Mother for Teaching me how to tie my sneaker
THOU ART My *Glory* and **THOU ART My** *Strength*
All the Blessing I Receive are Heaven Sent
THOU ART My *ALL and Everything*
You're the Reason I continue to <u>Dance</u> and <u>Sing</u>
THOU ART the *Most Highest of GODS*
Because **THOU ART** *the One, the Only,* <u>The True GOD!</u>

LETTER 2 GOD

Mother I come 2 you giving you the <u>Praise</u>
I come 2 you with my hands raised
Magnifying and Uplifting your **Wonderful Name**
This is the reason that I came
LORD 4give me 4 all the wrongs I've done
Wash me cleanses me until they're all gone
Hear O HEAVENS and lend your <u>Bionic Ear</u>
And listen 2 the **Sweet Words** you're about 2 hear
Bind up all the evil forces which try 2 come up against me
Take them down b4 they even reach me
Because the GRACE which you give is <u>Absolutely Free</u>
Which makes me want 2 be the best that I can be
A **Miraculous Blessing** is all a Brother needs
Come on LORD I got hungry mouths 2 feed
All the blessing I receive Come Directly from you
Because that's what the **GOOD BOOKS** say you do
Every day is a better attempt 2 be just like THEE
Thank you Mother 4 teaching me how 2 be, I mean be me
LORD why do so many people have 2 **Suffer and Struggle**
Would you pretty please Guide your people out of trouble?
The **Awesome Words** that I speak are **Spirit** and they are **Life**
They come at you cutting like the sharpest kitchen knife
Therefore I speak **PEACE, HAPPINESS** AND **JOY**
I just want 2 Thank the LORD 4 my little girls and my little boy
LORD Thanks 4 ***LOVE, WISDOM*** and Valuable ***KNOWLEDGE***
Even though I didn't go 2 Holy Cross or Bible College
LORD Thanks 4 Answering all my Prayers
Now that shows <u>You Really Care</u>
Because you never gave me more than I could bare
This Letter is 2 the **GOD of Heaven** the **GOD of Earth**
The GOD that Loved us all not **2**nd but **1**st**!**

Opportunity

What is **Opportunity** and when does it knock?
It's knocking now, trying to give you the keys to the padlock
Opportunity is what happens when you decide to move your
feet
So move, groove to that down south beat
And there's enough for all so there's no need to cheat
Don't you know you have to get out your little bitty box?
You never know, you might be the next Redd or Jamie Foxx
Opportunity doesn't knock and shout very loud
Sometimes it's hidden behind that dark cloud
Everyday gives you another chance
So if dancing is what you want to do, **Go Dance**
Just Be Ready for **Opportunity** when it comes
Don't be sitting around with your friends looking all-dumb
Because you never know, where **Mother Opportunity** is going
to **Spring Up** from
It's **Opportunity** saying, *"Come Get Yourself Some"*
So **Opportunity** I have to get to you
To every **Opportunity** Let me be True
Just tell me, which door do I go through!

Be A Light

Be a Light in a cold, dark and desolate land
Being a Light can Increase your Life span
GOD'S eyes are about 2 scan the land
Is your candle on the nightstand?
GOD said, "Let there be Light at the Beginning of Creation"
I made being a Light my main Occupation
Because it gives me the Greatest Sensation
Your Light might turn someone's Life around
Because Light Frees' those who are bound
Be a Light and get down on your knees
Because Prayer grows the smallest peas
Be a Light that never goes out
Good Words is what I shout
Shed your Light, with all your might
So the blind can receive their sight
The Candle Lighter is ready to LIGHT
As the day begins to overpower the night
Wrong gives way to the Right
Because someone chose to Be a Light
Not this little light of mine
But this Big Light of mine
Is what I'm going to let shine!

MY PRAYER

Kingdom of GOD will of GOD be Done
Please lend your Ear 2 your friend and 2 your Son
Guard me Guide me and most definitely **Feed me**
<u>4 all my Help I Know comes from Thee</u>
Show me what I ought and should be
Come on LORD give your boy a little peek see
GOD I know you are my <u>Every Footstep</u>
Along the way I know I'm going 2 need your help
I'm going out on thy ***Predestined Path***
So maybe I ought 2 take a shower or a bath
LORD I'm asking you 2 shake up this crazy earth
Because you been my Help and Strength from Mighty Birth
All I'm asking 4 is the Mothers Delicate Touch
Because I know that's not Asking 2 Much
Love my Family and **Love my True Friends**
MY PRAYER LORD is that they will <u>Endure 2 the End</u>
Hear **MY PRAYERS** from Heaven up Above
This is how I know you show me Love
Create in me a clean heart O'LORD
Because LORD you know I'm all yours
This is **MY PRAYER, MY PRAYER** 2 my LORD!

JUST ASK

GOD is Watching and Waiting for you to **Ask**
You must understand this is the **KEY** to the task
Ask everyday for the Mother's ***Delicate Touch***
Never, Never, think you're **Asking** too much
Ask and you shall receive
All GOD requires is for you to **BELIEVE**
To claim it, is to <u>State Exactly What You Want</u>
By not **Asking** what you're really saying is you don't
Though you (***Hear***) nothing She's Speaking
Though you (**See**) nothing She's Acting
Because GODS Mighty Blessing is ready- ready for the **Asking**
So **Just Ask** the Mother for the Answer to your Question
Just Ask no matter the occasion
By **Asking** you're putting everything into Motion
It's like rubbing your body down with <u>GOD'S Spiritual Lotion</u>
And it might be <u>The Only Way</u> to get that much deserved
Promotion
So **Just Ask,** *Come on Baabbie!* Don't hold back
Could that be the reason for your lack?
Because you have yet- yet to <u>ASK!</u>

INVEST IN ME!

It's time 4 a **Better Life** 4 you & me
Hey people <u>Togetherness is the Key</u>
All I'm asking 4 is one Opportunity
2 Bring a divided people <u>Together in Total Unity</u>
Investing In Me is going to put Revenues in your pocket
I'm your Electricity so plug in2 the Electrical Socket
Investing In Me is like Sweet <u>Money in the Bank</u>
I'm in GODS ARMY & from what SHE tells me *I Got High*
Rank
As the devil begins 2 walk down the plank
Because he refuses 2 thank
Jump on the train because I'm going 2 the Promised Land
And the only way 2 get there is 2 to hold Holy Hands
Every Woman Every Man
JOIN IN on GODS *Master Plan*
Investing In Me is <u>Investing in You</u>
Love because that's what you were Created 2 do
Love me as I Love you
Invest in what's True
My how your <u>Investment Grew</u>
Thanks 4 doing what the Spirit led you 2 do!

HOPE

There is **HOPE** for the Weary
Whose eyeballs are Teary
I **HOPE** because She helps me COPE
Who do you **HOPE** in GOD or an aging Pope?
HOPE sustains the very Fabric of Life itself
HOPE is what I pulled off the shelf
She is who I Love to read about
Like a pregnant women she pushed out my doubt
Her scream was a Mighty Shout
So keep Hoping for a Better Day
For more HOPE is what I Pray
Because **HOPE** always has something Good to Say
I **HOPE** therefore I Live
She is all I have to give
She keeps me on the Positive
HOPE can be seen in my eyes
My Belief caught the Devil by surprise
Like McDonalds Fries my **HOPE** has been Super Sized
Lose **HOPE** and shortly death will appear
Let these Words soothe your ear
Have New **HOPE** like a New Year
As I wait in Expectation
Because **HOPE** leaves the Greatest Impression
So let the World regain her **HOPE**
Or like the Cowboy go get a rope
Because you're as good as dead if you ever lose **HOPE!**

THROUGH MY SUFFERINGS

Out of Suffering comes the Strongest of Souls
We as **Black Folks** have experienced enough 2 fill a Giant Bowl
The reason 4 my Suffering I don't know
Hold up wait a minute that's how Life sometime goes
THROUGH MY SUFFERINGS I found out about the <u>Person called Self</u>
Come on LORD take it away b4 I have nothing left
I even sometimes come close 2 death
I learned GOD was just dusting off my Dirty Shelf
THROUGH MY SUFFERINGS I gained <u>Valuable Understanding</u>
4 Relief is what I started demanding
It's Healing coming in 4 the smoothest Landing
THROUGH MY SUFFERINGS I found out that the Mighty Sufferers
Turn out 2 be some of the **Best Comforters**
THROUGH MY SUFFERINGS I found out about the **True Me**
GOD was just showing me the person he wanted me 2 be
THROUGH MY SUFFERINGS THROUGH MY Unquenchable Suffering
I learned not 2 be the ONE causing the Sufferings
Thanks Suffering 4 making me Brand New
Because Adversity is how the Best are Grew
So we Suffer in order 2 know
Because pain pours down like December Snow
THROUGH MY SUFFERINGS GOD brought me safely Through
And SHE WILL DO IT 4 YOU 2!

JESUS

Jesus came to Save the least, the lost, and the last
Thank Goodness, He doesn't condemn us for our past
The Ministry of Jesus was one of Action and Authority
He shot through my body with a Surge of Electricity
And gave me the ability, to Speak with so much Intensity
He crept into my vicinity
It was Jesus who (Touched me)!
Jesus the Author of Time and can make up for all that was lost
Because He came died/rose and Paid the Final Cost
Which gives Him the Title of Supreme Boss
Jesus Christ the same Yesterday, Today and Forever
Choose Him and the whole world will know that you're clever
Because He promises to be down with you in any kind of weather
No matter how far down you think you are
The *Hand of GOD* can heal every broken scar
Because Jesus knows who you are
After all He placed you on the earth, like He placed one of His
Heavenly Stars
I said, "Jesus why are so many people falling through the cracks?"
He said, "Because Self-Intelligence is what they lack
Which will continue to hold them back"
But watch out because the Word of GOD is on the Attack
It's like a Magnet, It has the Power to Attract
The Blood of Jesus has Set us Free
It was His reason for hanging on the tree
For You and for Me, so the whole world could see
I Love Jesus because Jesus 1st Loved me
Thanks **Jesus** for doing what no other could
GOD sent You because He knew You would
Now Believing in **Jesus,** I tell you, It's All-Good!

Friends Forever

A Friend is someone you can Trust
So finding a True Friend is a big must
A Friend is someone who will Love You 4 You
And won't tell all the secret things you do
A Friend always refrains from saying the unkind and negative thing
My Friend makes me want 2 Sing
I hope it's **My Friend** when the phone begins 2 ring
<u>A Friend always keeps the promises that they make</u>
Friends Forever is what I'm trying 2 bake
Like a Beautiful, Birthday Cake
Be of the Realest Real and not the Fakest Fake
Or get Dee-Dee Teed by the wrestler Jake the Snake
Love your Family and Friends while you can
Because Tomorrow isn't promised 2 any man
My Assignment is 2 be the <u>Friendliest Man in all the land</u>
Because *Real Friends* always Understand
A Friend is **Forever**
Even if GOD decided to pull the death lever
Our Friendship, our Friendship will Last Forever
GOD will you Pretty Please be my **Best Friend**?
It's Forever so it will never, ever come to an End
Friends Forever means **Friends Forever**
I made GOD my **Best Friend**, so I'm Clever
A <u>Forever Friend </u>is who you be
I'm the Lock and GOD became the Key!

Grandma Mary Lee

Grandma Mary Lee has Come & Gone
2 her Everlasting Home
Grandma of the Year was inscribed on the Tombstone
Sit back as I Reminisce on my **Grandma Mary Lee**
Glory 2 GOD who sets the Spirit Free
<u>The Provider</u> 4 her Family is who she be
At least that's the way it looked 2 me
Slaving hanging live chickens at Tyson Foods
Which sometimes had her in a bad mood
I know our hearts are sad & some are mad
I know it looks bad the only Momma & Grandma some of us ever had
She's now with her Maker that <u>Great Spirit Taker</u>
Grandma Mary Lee made Thanksgiving & Christmas so Sweet
She kept her house Nice & Neat
She stepped in2 Heaven so she had 2 wipe her feet
Because her heart had beat its last beat
She tried her hardest 2 hold the <u>Family Together</u>
Through the often stormy weather
But she's gone 2 a place Far Better
<u>I want Grandma 2 Live</u> so I wrote this Letter
Grandma Mary Lee you is who we will miss
On her forehead GOD gave her a Heavenly Kiss
Be a Family was her Final Christmas Wish
Lois, Anthony, Tiffany, & San
Let's be a Family because we should & can
In Heaven is where Grandma now has 2 cook
Because she was listed in GODS Everlasting Good Book
So with that said **FAMILY** lets Rejoice
Because she's with GOD & her cakes were very moist
See you **Grandma Mary Lee** when we get there
Because when it comes 2 Grandmas there can be no spare
Go ahead **(Mary Lee Lee)** Get your Rest
As I imagine you on the Creators Chest
Talking about <u>He Loves the Best</u>
Congratulations! **Grandma Mary Lee** you Made It
The Angels are Singing & I can hear it
So Good Bye 4 now **Grandma Mary Lee**
From your Grandson Jimmy LEE!

The Disease of Depression

Depression has had its Mighty Hold on me
It wouldn't let me loose, it wouldn't set me Free
I was as Depressed as one could be
Too many tears made it hard 2 see
I tell you, Depression had me not wishing 2 live
What could I do when I was surrounded by so much
negative
No satisfaction does Depression give
Man being Broke make it Hard 2 Live
I remember when sleep was my best friend
Door closed so no one Gets In
I was locked in a Constant State of Depression
I was down in my Spirit is my Honest Confession
Living my Life in a Spiritual Recession
Boy Depression had me feeling sorry 4 myself
I was Hoping GOD would soon take my Breath
Without HOPE there's nothing Left
Because Life was kicking my Butt
Look at the Bruises, Look at the cuts
I must have cried an Ocean of Tears
Hey but some of my Peers been Depressed 4 years
The Cure 4 Depression is HOPE
Getting on Your Knees Hollering out 2 GOD will Help You
COPE
I PRAY 4 YOU because I KNOW Depression Ain't No Joke!

GOD'S Knocking

Hey can't you hear your GOD Knocking?
It has the geese and the goose flocking
And SHE'S making more noise than a punk rocker rocking
The devil is who SHE'S punching, upper cupping and socking
Mother Time has began Tic- Tocking
Broken hearts is what SHE'S sure to be unlocking
Will you hear the sound of HER Majestic voice?
Will opening the door be your 1st choice?
GOD says, "SHE knows you're in there"
SHE sees the TV (TV) glare
The GOD knocking I tell ya really cares
No one will be left out like in a game of Musical Chairs
If you hear HER Angelic voice
It's time to make your choice
Not opening could spell divorce
When it comes to Rappers I'm the Rolls Royce
Knock, knock, guess Who's Knocking at the Door
Open up the Door if your Heart is Sore
Some of you opened the door for the wrong person
So listen my friends to the Spiritual Surgeon
So Great Angel of Light do your thang
Let the Spring Time quickly sprang
I've been tattooed with your Spiritual Logo
Because I got Ancient Wisdom from long ago
Don't let that lower level devil wax up your ear
I got the alarm clock that drives out all the fear
As the Voice indicator is turned on
The knock BABBIE has me in a zone
Sorry there are no cracks in my Spiritual Crust

Because the Knock is what I began to Trust
So HEARTS be Extra Healed
Because that devils capped been peeled
Who's that beating at the door?
It's the one that loves you down to your core
Opening the door is your biggest must
Do it! Before you return to the Dirty Dust
So open up the flood gates of your soul
If you desire to be made whole
Like the SWAT Team GOD'S knocking down doors
Is the door She's knocking at yours?
Like the Mailman GOD pulled up at my home address
Ready to bless and relieve me from my Stress
Opening means the devils defeat
GOD'S knocking and it's bringing the heat
Don't knock anymore because you are my Dearest Friend
I hope the world gets the E-Mail I'm trying to send
GOD why are you knocking and you have the MASTER Key?
When all things belong to thee
So come on in and dine with me
Let that Liberated Spirit live in me
I was hypnotized by GODS Clever Conversation
So SHE inserted me into the Starting Rotation
GOD'S knocking and it sounds so Good
Not afraid to step in the hood
And SHE'S knocking for our good
You'll do it if you truly understood
I'm spreading my wings like a Colorful Peacock
Thanks BAABBIE for opening up to the True ROCK
And for believing in the KNOCK
Because my GOD is the TOP DOG on Every Block!

FAITH

A **Faith** that <u>Believes GOD</u> for anything can lift you up
A **Faith** like this will definitely pull you through the dirty dump
Faith only becomes Effective, when it becomes Active
So stop standing around, acting and being so passive
Speak your **Faith** and GOD will surely come through
Keep your Face to the Light and GOD will give you the Final Clue
Faith told me to tell you, "You can't be moved by what you See
Because what you Think You See, might not actually Be"
How I know, because that's what use to happen to me
Your **Faith** is your own Personal Fuel
So Fill HER to the Brim and all your friends will Think and Know that you're Cool
So ask that pretty girl or that handsome man out on a romantic date
Because a Believing **Faith,** I tell you, is all it's going to take
Do you have **Faith** or do you sit around and player hate?
Because you lack the necessary Faith
Watch out because **Faith** and I have JUST become running mates
Now that's who I asked out on a romantic date
Because **Faith** found out, I have what it takes
I Have <u>FAITH!</u>

Success

No one ever attains **Success** by simply doing what is required of him

Success usually comes to the one who is willing to step out on that Forbidden Limb

Each individual was created for Success

The Knowledge I'm passing on is Good and Profitable for business

I Love the Smell of Sweet **Success**

I got to be **Successful** and can't have it any less

It's been implanted In my Chest

Success to me is sweet as Fresh made honey

With **Success** comes that <u>Green Stuff we call Money</u>

Success is what Lights up and Illuminates the Human Soul

It Lights up every time a <u>Persistent</u> Brother reaches his number one Goal

The Secret to **Success** is to know something no one else knows

Unfortunately you're going to have to take a couple of Mike Tyson like, Knock Out Blows

And wait for GOD to Open up some closed Doors

Success comes to the one who pursues it

That's why **Success and I** have become the Perfect Fit

Now this is a message, **Too Legit to Quit**

Success *is* ***Knowing,*** <u>What You Want!</u>

And **Success** *is* ***Knowing,*** <u>What You Don't!</u>

I Said O'Lord

I Said O'Lord, would you have mercy on me
Lead me to that Special place, that's right next to Thee
I Said O'Lord, would you keep my Spiritual Lamp constantly Burning
To be more like you is what my heart's Yearning
Because from what I've seen, you're the only GOD going
With all those miracles you keep on showing
I Said O'Lord, could I have the Solution, I mean the Answer
Believe me; GOD has the Cure for every form of cancer
I Said O'Lord, would you pour out your Beautiful Spirit on me
So I can properly see, what you have for him/her and me
I Said O'Lord, could you give me a Wise and Understanding heart
That enables me to stop mess, before it starts
Give me my Spiritual Weapons like you gave Maxwell Smart
And Heal what Division has torn apart
I Said O'Lord, would you keep the Promises that you make
Because I'm hoping to see you at those Pearly Gates
I Said O'Lord, let Heaven be my Final Fate
Hear my Prayers, *O'Lord,* for Goodness Sake
And Thanks for showing up, not a moment too late
I Said O'Lord, can I speak your WORD
That's sharper than the Sharpest Sword
What I'm saying is I need your help O'Lord
That's what **I said O'Lord**
And give me something to do because I'm bored!

I Got 2 Make It

I Got 2 Make It, I have no other choice
That's why I'm standing up to be **GODS Voice**
I Got 2 Make It because <u>Winners Win</u>
That's why I'm here telling you where I'm going and where I've been
<u>A Risky Winner always starts off as Persistent Beginner</u>
I'm a sinner BUT I WAS MADE a natural born Winner
The world needs a brother like me
The pressure is on I got a lot of folks depending on me
If I don't make it who's going to help my family and closest friends
Because all they see is the deadly dead end
I Got to Make It and I'll tell you why
Because my steps are ordered by the **True GOD of the Sky**
Who's just leading me to my Gigantic piece of the American Pie
Why She choose me don't ask me why
To Jimia, Styles & Zaniah I want to say Hi
Shame on me, if I don't give this Speaking thing a Try!
Where I'm from there's nothing but unnecessary lack
With those Trained Haters trying 2 holding you back
Like JESUS I made GOD my ACE
You better BELIEVE, Poverty is what I'm here to erase
I Got 2 Make It so I burned all bridges
I got GOD and I don't mean to sound all-religious
Ain't no going back ain't no turning around
Because where I'm from no Success could be found
Which made me scudaddle to another town
So when I talk I don't mean to frown
But I'm hated on because the color of my skin
My Heritage is what I'm here to Defend
I like how Financial Freedom REALLY sound
I'm a KING and Kings don't hold their heads down
I made it to the land flowing with Honey and Milk
I'm overpowering poverty like leather over silk
Taking chances like the bear invading the bee's hive
Because oppression is swallowing (Swallowing) our people alive
I GOT 2 MAKE IT
AND I CAN'T SHAKE IT!

I'm Hungry

I'm Hungry because there's something that I lack
It's the constant struggle against the enemy who always tries to
hold me back
And the only food that will satisfy is sweet success
I expect the best got dam it and nothing less
Because **I'm Hungry HUNGRY** to be the Best
Nourish me like milk coming from the Mothers Breast
<u>When I Speak</u> the people will **Rejoice**
Because the Delicious devil is the main course
These Mighty Hunger pains have been going on for a long
time
Because I'm constantly getting hog tied by white collar crime
I refuse to eat your Bible of Rotten Lies
<u>You kidnapped us from Africa,</u> which broke all family ties
Our people will no longer be foolishly misled
We're Kings and Queens but you have us living like Jethro and
Jed
We're **Spiritually Weak** because we haven't been properly fed
And we ain't taken any more and I hope you heard what I said
I Got my Fork and my Spoon in my Hand
Feed Me, Feed Me is what I Now Demand!
I was Food Poisoned by <u>Digesting Lies</u> and not Truth
It's what I'm proclaiming in the broadcast booth
I'm So Hungry man I can hardly sleep at night
So I must bring the **Truth (Truth)** to the Light
You devils know what you love to do
All the mess-ups of the world are because of you
You love the fake & **you hate the True**

Who do you think I am Willie Foo Foo
You're a Pepsi that's lost it suds
You're a flower that won't bud
Like the bully I just pushed the devil in the mud
When it comes to Spirituality I'm a Super Stud
I'm So Hungry I could eat a horse
But chicken would be my **1st choice**
GOD delivered me a Full Course Meal
Don't starve me because I don't like how it makes me Feel
I Got my Fork and my Spoon in my Hand
Feed Me, Feed Me is what I Now Demand
I think I smell something cooking in the kitchen
Just make sure the **hot sauce** isn't missin
GOD supplied the breakfast, lunch and the dinner
Which hit my Center
GOD just Opened up the Treasures of my pantry door
Finding food is my daily chore
Feed my Body and Spirit what it needs
Let me be filled with Awesome and GOOD deeds
Satisfying People's Hunger is what GOD is all about
I'm FULL is the reason that I shout
My stomach no longer sounds like Thunder
Because Starvation even took the Cookie Monster Under
GODS Lyrics are Great to the Taste Buds
In the group of the Satisfied is what I'm Of
GOD did it for me and She'll do it for you
Because I know you Hungry Too!

Depressed on the Inside

My Spirit is down wearing an upside down frown
I see depression in every town
No laughter from the clown
Because he 2 is feeling down
In his agony of despair because no one seems 2 care
Life giving him, me & you all we can bare
Like a Short Poem or a Short Song
My Happiness if it comes at all doesn't last very long
I'm talking about being Stressed & Depressed
My pain can no longer go Unconfessed & Unexpressed
I'm Depressed on the Inner Inside
Its gloom has reach my Outer Outside
Circumstances got me Confused in my mind
Hopelessness continues 2 dull my shine
My insides are Damaged & Beyond Hurting
Cause nothing in my Life is properly working
My Tormented Soul Cry's from *Deep Within*
If I'm smiling it's an <u>Empty Grin</u>
O if I could just sleep my life away
Maybe that will make everything ok
But when I wake up life is still <u>Rough & Tough</u>
Hey that's when I said **Enough is Enough**
So depression I'm calling your bluff
I done taken enough of your stuff
I'm* <u>Overcoming</u> *this disease
So I hollered LORD <u>Help me Please</u>
Send me a Cool Breeze while I'm on my knees
I need some Money! I need some Cheese!
Didn't you hear me I said <u>Please?</u>
My mind has been **Renewed**
That ends my Family Feud
My Inside depression has come 2 an end
Because I finally let <u>Healing In!</u>

GOD Wants The Attention!

GOD wants the attention I had to mention
This is my petition to get your attention
It's time to give GOD Her due
That's to every one of you
Pray because it's the half time intermission
GODS coming down so She's making Her dissension
If GOD isn't real it was the Perfect Invention
The Center of Attention is what GOD what's to be
It's my only plea
Because GOD holds the key
Like 2pac said, **"All Eyes On Me"**
GOD just wants the Energy that you give
Because the Queen is who She Is
In the Royal court is where She dwells
Sit back because I have many stories to tell
GODS here and She's leaving a trail
So eat the Fresh and Spit out the stale
Talking about GOD is what I Love to do
And the Praises of GOD are far from being a few
Thanks GOD for letting me be a part of your crew
You'll Know it was all GOD before I'm through
GOD just wants to feel Appreciated
Somehow we deviated
And that's something GOD hated
So this lack of attention must be vindicated
So the Navigator navigated
And to GOD the People Gravitated
I have Confidence in my Maker

That Back Breaker, Breath Taker
World Shaker, Revelation Baker
And that's from his devil sneaker
Loudest Speaker, Crowd Pleaser
And there's none <u>Meeker</u>
Hey I'm the Perfect GOD SEEKER
GOD wants the Attention I had to Mention
This is my Petition to get your Attention
<u>GOD'S the Chief Commander in Charge</u>
And She's Larger than Large
In every garage and on Every river barge
HER you cannot dodge
Or retreat to your hidden lodge
GOD to You I give the Glory
I'll do it so don't you worry
I'm coming at the people like a snow flurry
Because you're the <u>Author of this Story</u>
About giving **GOD the Glory**
It's not about me it's all about You
To the GOD I call The True
Which is nothing New
Through me LORD do what you do
Just let me <u>Speak for You</u>
Because <u>Heaven is what I want to get into</u>
Come to GOD, Come to GOD is what I cry
As I look above to the Most High
We're so close we're connected at the hip
Because we have the <u>Perfect Relationship</u>
<u>LOOK at GOD</u> and stop gazing at me
My GOD is all I want you to see

Great Creator let your Kingdom Come
Divide the breadcrumb, erase every hater and Uncle Tom
I know you <u>LOVE ALL</u> and not just some
<u>Refresh the World</u> like a new pack of bubble gum
Whether Smart or Dumb, Rich or Bum
Give GOD some, before your heart becomes numb
It's time to make your Final Decision
Because our Mighty QUEEN has Finally Arisen
<u>This has been My Petition to Get Your Attention!</u>

THE TRUTH

THE TRUTH is what I'm searching 4
THE TRUTH about the Rich THE TRUTH about the
Poor
Will TRUTH please tally up the Final score?
We really think we know THE TRUTH
Who was the Best Jackie Robinson or Babe Ruth?
I'm still trying 2 figure it all out
Why we're hated so much here in the Dirty South
It only seems like yesterday that we were living like slaves
Like a Resurrected Jesus TRUTH is walking out the cave
The path that leads to TRUTH is what I'm trying 2 pave
O'LORD please HELP me 2 be Brave
I come to you GOD because you're the BOSS
Spread TRUTH like Louisiana Hot Sauce
This is my outcry 4 THE TRUTH
Because falsehood hurts like a decaying tooth
Life got me wishing I were dead
Because I got all these Questions running through my head
The Whole TRUTH is what I anticipate
It has my heart pumping at the Highest rate
Do me a Favor GOD and put falsehood to bed
I want TRUTH and I Hope you heard what I said
Getting 2 Her is a Musty Must
Because she is the only one who can satisfy my Thirst
So watch out THE TRUTH is about 2 Burst
Because I BELIEVED in THE TRUTH 1ST!

I'M RICH BUT!

I have all the things in this world I can ask 4
So why I'm I busting my butt trying 2 get more?
This issue is what I'm going 2 explore
Because I feel rotten 2 the core
I have 6 brand new luxury cars
But that's not enough 2 conceal my **Emotional Scars**
This is the **Life of Millionaires** & **Superstars**
I'm Free but Money has me locked behind bars
I have women over here & dime pieces over there
That would make a blind man stare
I'm Rich But I'm not really HAPPY
Because I must follow in the footsteps of dear old pappy
And I don't sleep well at night
Because I'm under the worlds Microscopic light
I'm Rich But everything is not Alright
You who think it's easy being rich can go fly a kite
Your mind is what I'm about to sew & stitch
4 True Happiness would you switch?
The rich get sick 2 just like me & you
On my Richness take a chew
Because this is what the Rich go through
People begging 4 handouts
As new kinfolks begin 2 Spring & Sprout
The Rich know what I'm talking about
Remember **I Got Money** 2 burn
But on the **Beds of Luxury** I still toss &turn
I'm Rich But money got the best of me
Just like it got the best of karate expert Bruce Lee
So being Rich is not all it's cracked up 2 be
There is one thing that will set the Rich Free
<u>Give</u> & a **Liberated Soul** is what you will be
2 the Rich I Hope you hear my plea
From selfishness you need 2 flee
Or Don't you have the Heart 2 Truly See!

Proverbs of a King

When the **KING** sits on his throne 2 Judge
With the *Wisdom of GOD* he cannot be Budged
And he winnows out all evil with his eyes
He shall see the Glory of his **LORD** B4 he dies
As GOD intervenes in the Peoples Cries
A **KINGS** wrath is like the Roar of a **Mighty Lion**
So don't come 2 the **KING** with your deceit & lying
He who Angers him forfeits his life
So you better be Good, you better do right
He is a fool who foolishly abuses his wife
Love & Faithfulness keep the **KING** safe & Secure
As long as his Motives are Just & Pure
The **KINGS Proverbs** REVIVE the Soul
Making his people Complete & Whole
GOD has the **KING'S** Heart in His Hand
As Mother Love Promises him a Long Life Span
Because his foundation wasn't built on quick sand
Can't you see a **KING'S** Decree
Is packed with *GODS Authority*
The **Kingdom of GOD** has come so sound the Alarm
And HE comes holding his **KING** by the Arm!
What the **KINGS** says is Supreme
But a **KING** is nothing without his **TEAM**
Like Martin Luther King lets **DREAM!**

How's Your Thinking

What a man Thinks is what he will be
<u>Thoughts are Things</u> that you can see
The Greatest BATTLES are fought in the Mind
GOD has given use the Power 2 loose or bind
Think Kind instead of Unkind
Think your way up out your bind
In this poem the Truth is what you're going to find
So let your Thoughts begin 2 Speak
Depression causes the Mind 2 leak
You can be Strong or you can be weak
<u>Good Thinking</u> is the reason 4 my Winning Streak
And watch out 4 what you put in your head
Or you'll be a King but living like Jethro and Jed
Who was a sped
Because his Mind would not get out the bed
Hey your Thinking is how you are lead
<u>Think Positive</u> is what this poem said
The Devil is searching for Minds he can bruise and scar
Because he knows who you are
Thoughts are the Seeds of Action
Keep Thinking it and you're sure to get a reaction
So I'm asking you to <u>Change the way you Think</u>
If you understand give GOD a wink
And use your <u>Mind for Good</u>
You would if you Truly Understood
Thinking is only part of the Test
When you get older, I'll tell you the rest
But be sure 2 Think<u>(THINK) YOUR BEST!</u>

Be a Winner

I was once asked what does it take to be a **Winner**
I said, "You can't win unless you start off as a beginner
It's the person that wakes up every morning
Breathe smelling bad while he's yarning
But his mind is set on what he's doing
And he really knows where he's going
Because he knows, **Winning** is all about showing
And his face is ***Confident and Glowing***
To be a winner you must 1st have a <u>Winner's Mentality</u>
The knowledge I'm passing on is all reality
Try being a **Winner** in your Nightly Dreams
Just do it, no matter how crazy it may seem
When you begin to lose, please wake up and scream
Because you don't want to be on the losers team
<u>Hanging around Winners will surely help you Win</u>
That's why **Winning** and I have become close friends
Because **I'm a Winner** and a **Winner's job is to win**
Because to me losing is the only sin
So tell me when does the fun begin?
Be a Winner in your mind
It's the only way to get out your bind
Because **Winners** produce after their own kind
Be a Winner is the song that I sang
Because Victory lets loose the Biggest Bang!

Football Taught Me

Football is Game I once Loved 2 play
I'm coming down hill so you better Pray
As the receiver hollers May Day
& He woke up the next day thinking he was gay
Jerry Rice not Jerrika Rice was what he was trying 2 say
<u>Thank Goodness</u> he had a mother who loved 2 pray
Football is a game that <u>Taught Me</u> a lot about life
It <u>Taught Me</u> how 2 back paddle away from the nagging wife
We beat a team so bad one time the coach wanted 2 pull out a pocket knife
Now that wasn't Very Nice
<u>Football Taught Me</u> how 2 Study & how 2 Prepare
& Told me that **Pride** & **Honor** were the Perfect Pair
Like Tennessee's **Quarterback** *Steve McNair*
<u>Football Taught Me</u> about being a Family & about being a *Team*
& 2 never give up but 2 always *Pursue Your Dreams*
As the crowd begins 2 scream
In **Football** you're going 2 have your ups & your downs
But when Game Time comes my heart begins 2 Pump & Pound
As I listen 2 the crowd & those Friday Night sounds
In High School we <u>Won 51 Games</u> in a row
But I lost my last one though
I never want 2 lose my last again
Life just like **Football** will definitely break you in
Over Confidence was our Greatest Sin
<u>Pride Teamwork Dedication</u> is what it's going 2 take
& Believe in yourself & have a little Faith
& Catch a couple of *Lucky Breaks*
In **Football** you're going 2 have some Good Days & some bad days
But remember that **Hard Work** & **Commitment** will always pay
Life just like **Football** has given me my share of Bumps & Bruises
& <u>Taught Me</u> that the person who doesn't Prepare usually loses
Football is a Game where only the *Strong Survive*
The Pains of Life & **Football** let me know I'm still Alive
As Life throws me a High5
Football not my daddy *Taught Me*
Football was Good 4 me can't you see
Now kick that off your Kicking Tee
Because **Football**, <u>Football Taught Me!</u>

Teacher, Teacher

Teacher, Teacher, will you pretty please <u>Instruct</u> and <u>Teach</u> me
Will you Help me, be the person I'm supposed to be?
<u>I know you're not paid, what you should!</u>
But this might be my only way, out this broken down Neighborhood
Teacher, Teacher, I'm sorry, I don't mean to misbehave
But my daddy beats me and his name is Truck Driver Dave
I can Feel and Sense that you're having a very bad day
But I can't help it I got something very important to say
Teacher, Teacher, don't fret or worry about your Low and Degrading pay
GOD, told me to tell you, "Continue to Believe and Continue to Pray"
I'm here because I just want you to know
You're the reason I want to come to school even when it snow
Teacher, Teacher, would you pretty please be my <u>Positive Role Model?</u>
Because if you don't, I might have to turn to the Mighty Wine Bottle
Teacher, Teacher, Thanks for Assisting me in the Game of Life
You Taught me, <u>How to Read</u> which gave me ***Abundant Life***
Beautiful Teachers, I realize that you do so much
That's why my Prayer to GOD is, that he would **Bless You,** I mean
<u>BLESS YOU</u> a Bunch!
And I'm shouting it from the loudest speaker
Because *Teacher, Teacher,* you are **My** <u>Favorite Teacher!</u>

MAN I'M STRUGGLING

Everything seems to be coming at me all at the same time
The bills are due and I don't have a dime
And a brother is wondering will I have 2 turn 2 a life of crime
Because time is ticking time seems 2 be running out
STRUGGLE makes a Grown Man want 2 cry and shout
Some of you men know what I'm talking about
Everybody **STRUGGLING** trying 2 make ends meat
But you can't make it unless you make the Effort 2 get up out your
Comfort Seat
As the **Tester of Life** turns up the heat
Man I thought I had this life thang beat
People working at jobs they just don't like
Just like me working at Wal-Mart a job I really liked Skye!
Baby mommas got the wrong baby daddies all on child support
Maybe it's time 2 take this issue 2 the Peoples Court
Women making tough choices 2 abort
But when the women gets pregnant that was suppose 2 be a Good
report
Everybody **STRUGGLING** trying 2 make a decent living
The reason everybody **SRUGGLING** is because <u>No Ones Sharing and</u>
<u>No Ones Giving</u>
This **STRUGGLING** thing has taught me a lot about life
That's probably the reason I don't have a wife
Because Life just ain't been Nice
STRUGGLING because death has taken my best friend
And I'm wondering LORD is this misery going 2 ever end
STRUGGLING, STRUGGLING could this be the reason every ones
Scheming and hustling
MAN I'M STRUGGLING
BUT

It Will Be Alright

Every Adversity, Every Failure, Every Heartache carries with it a
Greater Benefit
Sometimes I wonder is all this Drama Heaven Sent
It Will Be Alright
I know your favorite son is locked up in Hell, Oh I mean Prison
But it's not up to you or me it's GOD'S Ultimate Decision
It Will Be Alright
I know you're tired of working for $6.00 an hour
So let's Come Together, then we'll have Supreme Power
It Will Be Alright
I know you're long time boyfriend or husband left you with your Heart
all Broken
But in order for Healing to come in, the heart must remain Open
It Will Be Alright
You say you lost your daughter to Big Nasty Cancer
I'm sorry Momma, but only GOD has the Reason and the Answer
It Will Be Alright
I know you're wondering if GOD really Hears a person like You
I'm here to tell you, SHE Surely - Surely Do
I Promise You! <u>Everything is Going To Be Alright</u>
Just do me a Favor and Pray to GOD with all your Might
Because I found out, Prayer is what makes things right, Alright
Man, I'm struggling, but It Will Be Alright

From the Bottom to the Top

From the Bottom to the Top is my motto
Because this is how my Life is about to go
Zumm, zumm you must make room
As the devil meets his doom
So I'm hollering boom, boom
When it comes 2 Rhyming I'm an All Star and an All Pro
Like Michael Jackson this is a One Man Show
So Hello Showtime at the Apollo
As I tickle your taste buds with my Freestyle Flow
Because of the Mental Muscles that I Flex
I'm in the Upper Decks, Signing Million Dollar Checks
I Pack more Power than the Atomic Bomb
GOD is Smart and the devil is Dumb
To be the Best is what I claim
That means I'm the MVP of the game
And I hope I don't have to say it again
So are you out or in
Foe or Friend
My bags are packed and I'm ready to go
I'm spreading my wings out like a picked out Afro
So open up the doo
As I escape like the Mighty Joe
Because it's time to grow
Because I've been on the bottom for too long
To stay here would be my only wrong
Like the space shuttle I'm Lifting Off
Because I'm spicier than Tabasco hot sauce
Where I am is not where I want to be
At the top of the mountain is all I want to see
Where the white folks love to ski
At the Top of the Tree there's a picture of me
And it looks like that boy Jimmy Lee
Like lost dinosaur bones
All my haters are long gone
GOD is the only reason I got it going on
Up, Up, Up, Up, Up, Up an Away

I'm going to the top so get out the way
I've been planted and watered by the Good Gardner
Who became my closest partner
Jesus was GODS Greatest Martyr
Devils are who I'm here to tie up and slaughter
GOD operated on my mind like a Prime Time Doctor
As I kick my Words through the goal like they do in soccer
From the bottom to the Top
I'm here to change the game of Hip Hop
On the way to the Top
I'm licking on my strawberry or cherry Lolly Pop
The air is much better at the Top
But the only way to get there is to get off the pot
As Life Maneuvers me to the Right Spot
With Lyrics & Rhymes that are hotter than hot
Up, Up an Away, Up, Up an Away
I'm going to the top so get out the way
Like the giraffe my head hangs high
I'm confident and far from being shy
Move over and let me give this **SHOWBIZ** thing a try
I soared so high I had to learn to fly
The Top is where I want to be
I was drowning and GOD lifted my head above the Mighty Sea
And said She had something just for me
And there was no background check or application fee
Because the Master plan is what I got
I Hope you got your tacney shot
Reconstruction has been done on my behalf
With GODS Rod and Staff
I grew UP into a Mighty Bull from a Baby Calf
And that's not half
As I take my Spiritual Bath
It's like I'm from another planet like Alf
Up, Up an Away, Up, Up an Away
I'm going to the top so move out the way
On the way to the Top wasn't easy
A lot of people treated me kind of skezzy
It was stormy, it was breezy

But <u>Being the Best</u> is never easy
From the bottom to the Top
I got bubbles to pop
So I'm getting out my broom and my mop
The nonsense must stop, from the gangsters to the cop
As their heads drop
As they pull out of GODS body and mind shop
From the Top there's a Better View
Where things are New
But at the TOP there are only a Few
Will that few be you?
Excuse me for having a Giants Mentality
Watch as MY WORDS defy reality
Up, Up an Away, Up, Up an Away
I going to the top so get out my way
I was Baptized in Poverties Tears
On the way to the Top I had to conquer many fears
As GOD prunes me with HER Man Making Shears
To Outlast all my peers
I stopped shopping at wal-mart to shop at Sears
Because wal-mart been doing wrong for years
So I switched gears, like Santa's reindeers
Let these Prophetic Words penetrate your Mind and Ears
Because I'm the Best Rapper to come along since the 2pac Years
I'm the Diamond in the Ruff and the Cream of the Crop
The people are hollering my name from the rooftop
Now I got ya begging for more
As the Melodies continue to pour
The Winning Touchdown is what I scored
I Thank GOD because I'm no longer bored
From the bottom is where I'm coming from
On my Toppness get yourself some!

LEARNING

LEARNING is a everyday task
As I take a peep at what's behind the mask
In the **Sunshine's of WISDOM** I embrace
And it can be seen all over my face
By the way you look I can tell you won the race
Because the Anointing always leaves a trace
I'm just a man who **Desires 2 Understand**
Who's not afraid 2 Take a Stand
As GOD lets loose my Daily Lesson Plans
LEARNING 2 do this and not 2 do that
And I'm knowing falsehood smells like a dirty rat
I Thank GOD 4 the ability 2 Learn
Look at the battle scars I've earned
The Teacher is Tough Fair and Stern
I'm in Gods' hand so I don't have 2 burn
Learn all you can is what my Savior said
Put Good Things in your Head
On the Breakfast of **LEARNING** is how I'm fed
You can't Learn if you don't listen
I saw Wisdom and Love kissing
4 more Knowledge and Understanding is what I'm wishing
I live 2 Learn it's my only concern
And what I Learn I Live
I THANK GOD 4 the lessons She gives
They seem 2 make me Stronger
Satisfying my Spiritual Hunger
With the Ability 2 Ponder and Wonder
As I pull the Gates of Truth Asunder!

QUESTIONS?

All these **Questions** I have running through my mind
Trying 2 figure out a way up out this financial bind
That big old monkey is putting extra pressure on my spine
Why does the enemy come against me & mine?
So LORD will you Answer my **Questions**?
Get away devil cause your breath smell like old onions
Where do we go when we die?
Why do tears cry?
How does Prayer Work?
Will we ever come together in **Total Teamwork**?
Is it wrong or right to consume swine or pork?
Was <u>JESUS CHRIST</u> really GOD?
Why does life have 2 be so hard?
Which religion do I believe & Trust in?
How much sleep do I need 8 or 10?
Is it wrong 2 express how you truly feel?
Whose being fake & whose being real?
What is the right career PATH 4 me?
How far do you extend your Mercy?
When are things in my life going 2 Get Better?
Will you Answer my **Questions** in this letter?
Will you O'LORD manifest yourself b4 it's 2 late?
You Answering these **Questions** is what I anticipate!
Bark where ever you see a **Question Mark**
Just please answer O'LORD the Questions I have in my Heart!

Take a Walk, Take a Walk

Take a Walk, Take a Walk, Take a Walk with me
And let me tell you what I see
Taking walks is something I love to do
It helps me to think when I'm constantly going through
So **Take a Walk, Take a Walk** with me
And racism and discrimination is all you're going to see
Because the people are as Divided as can be
The heat has me hiding under the shade tree
Take a Walk, Take a Walk, down your favorite street
Take a Walk because there's no telling whom you're going to meet
All the youngsters are packing the heat
And stealing the shoes off each other's feet
With hair nappier than that boy Buckwheat
Take a Walk, Take a Walk, so you can check out the scene
Take a look at Mother Nature if you want to know what life really means
People surviving on stale bread and Pork & Beans
One side of town is dirty and the other side is clean
One with rich folks and the other with dope fens
Take a Walk, Take a Walk so you can cry a little bit
Just be careful not to step in someone else's ----
As my Walking Words begin to spit
In poverty and pain is where the poor people sit
The Truth is ready to be lit
Take a Walk, Take a Walk, with someone you admire and love
There's room to walk so don't push and shove
There's nothing wrong with walking with you Heavenly Father who sits high
above
The streets of Heaven is what I'm of
Talk and Walk, Talk and Talk
Just don't forget to **Take Your Walk**
So you can see another dead body outlined with white chalk
Take a Walk, Take a Walk, Take a Walk with me
Now after *Taking your Walk,* Tell me <u>What Do You See?</u>
Are we bound or are we free
We're locked down if you have eyes that see!

Drugs In My Hood
So Things Don't Look So Good

Why is my hood filled with crime and drugs?
And Patrolled by corrupt cops and thuggin thugs
Will someone please give these boys a hug?
Because they're dirtier than their momma's nasty rug
Narcotics and Drugs popping up everywhere I look
On the stove is where the crack man loves to cook
She's doing blow and she's only 13
Just another tricked out dope feen
Division and Racism slowing down our progress
When will our Savior relieve us from this stress?
Gunshots going off in the East & the West
So we can't sleep we can't rest
We live in the worst and not the best
This is the world of the tortured and oppressed
The struggling the deprived and the depressed
I tell ya Poverty is a PEST
Like Inspector Gadget I'm searching for Good in my Hood
I know you would leave if you could
I'm Broke so I'm stuck in the Hood
Was I born on the wrong side of town?
The side for the black and the brown
The economic economy has us chained and bound
The stress is causing my heart to lose its pound
Because we're being Controlled by the #1 controllers
The Gov't styling us like hair rollers
When will they cut our people some slack?
And stop trying to hold us back
Everyone hustling trying to make a buck

To make it out the hood they call it luck
Our neighborhood produces bad ass little Chuckey's
Sticky finger Dope heads and future flunkies
They call us apes they call us Monkey's
Like Malcolm X we've been run a muck
We're divided is the reason we're stuck
The devils doing everything to steal our clout
But I'm turning the Truth inside out
Drugs in my Hood
So Things don't look so Good
Our Kids are going to school with no money in their pocket
We're like a TV without an electrical socket
Like the Great Depression times are so Hard
Come on people it's time to come to GOD
Togetherness in the hood is what we need
I'm the Leader so BAABBY follow my lead
Survival is the name of the game
So I'm not going to fuss or complain
Because there's no need to throw blame
When I get through the hood won't be the same
My hood is filled with so much pain
With noisy choo -choo trains
The Avenues of my Brain is what I use
Standing Up for my hood is what choose
I speak in Love so how can I lose?
I was sent here to get this ---- right
For my hood I'm here to fight
So in the hood things are getting better
Because we finally chose to come together
Now it's all Good in the Hood!

I DON'T KNOW

I DON'T KNOW why I hated 4 the color of my <u>Unchangeable skin</u>
Is it because that's what you been taught by your closes of kin
Wouldn't it be much easier just 2 be friends?
I DON'T KNOW why people we love have 2 die
Is it because there's a better place waiting in the sky
Not knowing makes me want 2 cry
I DON'T KNOW why GOD Loves me so much
I DON'T KNOW about you but I felt the ***Mothers Gentle Touch***
I DON'T KNOW why GOD would choose a person like me
All I know is She gave Her boy a new set of keys
And told me ***GO BE ALL YOU CAN BE***
I DON'T KNOW what makes a man want 2 cheat
I don't think he'd do it if he heard your ***Precious Heart Beat***
I DON'T KNOW why GOD would create and make a burning hell
Is it because silly man just wanted a Good Story 2 tell
I DON'T KNOW why they'd want 2 kill King Jesus
I bet it was because he was 4 poor old us
But what they done makes me want 2 cuss
I DON'T KNOW everything I need 2 know
I just know this is not how life is suppose 2 go!

What I See

I See things 4 what they Really Are
Every time we catch up they seem 2 *raise the bar*
I See **Education** & **Recreation** at the top of every Budget Cut
Then you wonder why our **Children** & **Schools** are in an all time rut
I See 2 many of my **Black Brothers** in the streets are dying
That's the reason so many **Depressed Mothers** on their knees crying
I See so much racism & hatred in my Mayberry looking town
Then you wonder what makes a brother want 2 act a fool & make a
Brother want 2 Clown
I See so many *Innocent People* in Unbearable Pain
See in the **Black Man's World** it always seems 2 Rain
It's enough 2 Drive a grown man Insane
Then I get 2 wondering is all this <u>Drama Preordained?</u>
I See a President who Loves 2 start **Useless Wars**
Acting like he's Cowboy Bill Watts pretending 2 be Hardcore
I See so many *Delinquent* & *Overdue* bills
I'm already knowing I'm going 2 have 2 miss a couple of Hot meals
Ah but *I See* a *Brighter Day on the Horizon*
A day when all of <u>GODS Children</u> are going 2 be able 2 have some fun
I See the wicked being destroyed & losing his power
So Rejoice <u>Good People</u> this is <u>Your Hour of Divine Power</u>
I See a lot of things out of order
But what I also see is the devil making a run 4 the border
Now that's what <u>I Jimmy Lee SEE</u>
Tell me, What Do You See?

UNITE or DIE

Coming Together is the key 2 the Victory
It's what all the Greats have Preached all down through history
Where did we begin 2 turn from that Glorious Light
Holding hands with your Brother & Sister makes the Future so bright
Division is what brings about the Deadly Death
If you truly want **2 Live** you need to get off self
Going 2 war by yourself is a sure sign you're ready 2 die
And GOD is sitting in Heaven saying My, My, My
Coming Together 4 something that you know is right
But all silly man wants to do is *fuss & fight*
About who's wrong & who's right
Uniting is what brings about *Perfect Peace*
Now that's what I'm always telling my little niece
Uniting is 4 the GOOD of MAN
That's why I'm up here doing all I can
2 get silly man 2 Understand
A **Team**, a **Church**, a **Family**, a **Nation** Divided cannot & will not stand
Just Take a look around if you have yet 2 understand
Unite or Die & don't ask me why
Unite or Die or we all fixing 2 fry
Unite or Die because I just told you why!

TEAMWORK!

TEAMWORK is the <u>Greatest Need of the Hour</u>
Because with it we Generate so much Supreme Power
With **TEAMWORK** a *Touchdown* is what you're sure 2 Score
And when it rains it pours
Great Champions know all about **TEAMWORK**
That's why at the end of the Season they always popping
Champagne Corks
If you want 2 **WIN** this is where you Start
But remember EVERYONE must do his or her part
I'm telling you **TEAMWORK** is Smarter than Smart
I Believe in its **Power** with all my Heart!
TEAMWORK will never be found on the loser's side
That's why **TEAMWORK** is the only way I ride
TEAMWORK is just another Word 4 **UNITY**
It's what makes a People a Community
I'm doing this because this is my Duty
So be a <u>TEAM PLAYER</u> like Notre Dames Rudy
TEAMWORK Try It I bet it Works
Because with **TEAMWORK** it has its Perks
TEAMWORK is *NEEDED* so stop acting so Conceited
Because with it Tell Me How Can WE be Defeated!

Division Go Away!

<u>Division Go Away!</u> you're not wanted here anymore
Because all you do is make the peoples booty sore
2 me you're nothing but a stinky whore
So I'm robbing you of all your power
You smell bad so go hit the shower
As I drop you from the highest Tower
Separation & **Division** is all I see
In a land where no one is allowed 2 be free
Because *Discrimination* is still messing with me
Everybody clicked up in his or her own little click
Man it's like Watching a horror flick
Discrimination is something we all need 2 kick
Because it's the devils main trick & he thinks he's slick
That's why Unity is my #1 pick
<u>Division Go Away!</u> because you're in the way
You done out stayed your stay
We need 2 slang division 2 the side
Division get your ass up out my ride
Because I found out you were on the loser's side
I'm telling you People I saw division when it died
Black & *White* people we need 2 come 2gether
That's the only way 2 calm the Stormy Weather
We need each other 2 make this <u>World Better</u>
This Generation must be the New Trendsetter
<u>DIVISION IS STUPID!</u>
So I'm hitting you with LOVE because I'm Cupid
LOVE came & division hid
Because it was something we all had 2 get rid
I'm putting you in the trashcan so where's the lid
As GOD Purchase division with the Highest Bid
<u>Division Go Away!</u> with yo OLD Ugly Self
You don't even know your right hand from your left
So I'm putting you back on the shelf
And don't let GOD have 2 take your breath
I'm sending you back 2 where you belong cause your wrong
The people are now singing a New Song
I saw you fall like the Love struck King Kong
Who lost his last ding-dong
<u>Division Go Away!</u> is what I Pray
And I mean 2day & don't you delay
Because we have NEW Foundations 2 lay
Division is Dead! & That's all I have 2 say
Because <u>Mr. UNITY</u> is here 2 save the day!

Be Positive

A Positive People is who we need to be
It makes us Beautiful can't you see
<u>Be Positive</u> when situations look bleak
By being Positive you will get those things, which you seek
Remember your mind controls the outcome
Where do you think the world came from?
Positive Energy is what we need to be giving off
Because it makes the hard, soft
So have the Right Attitude
Little Dude and don't be rude
Or off the stage you will be booed
Hit with Oranges and food
<u>Be Positive</u> when you're in your darkest hour
Sing Positive songs while you're in the shower
Because it gives us Supernatural Power
And it brings a smile to GOD'S Face
It's the only way to Win the race
That's why, Positive people is who I chase
Just like GODS Mercy and GODS Grace
Choose to Live in the Positive
If you wish to truly Live
Good Vibrations is what you give
When you make a decision to <u>Be Positive</u>
So do what I say young man
If you understand *GODS Divine Plan*
Like Moses on <u>Positive Ground</u> is where you need to stand
Because **Positivity** is the only way to make it to the Promised Land!

GET BETTA BAA'BBIE

GET BETTA BAA'BBIE is the Word of the Century
I Love what it does 4 U & I Love what it does 4 Me
May Improvement come our way is what I PRAY
We're **GETN BETTA** so It's a **GREAT GREAT DAY**
So I'm hollering Hip Hip HORRAY
Because I'm Much BETTA than I was Yesterday
Look Everybody's **GETN BETTA** in the land
GET BETTA BAA'BBIE is what I nicely Demand
Hey **GETN BETTA** is a part of GODS Master Plan
So come on, Boy, Woman Girl & Man
Going Forward is what we're about to do
2gether there's nothing we can't do
GETN BETTA makes us Feel Brand New
Yes My Friends my Words are talking Directly 2 U
If we **GET BETTA** in our Heart & Mind
Then our Life will Brightly Brightly Shine
So **GET BETTA BAA'BBIE** is what I loudly Scream
You & I **GETN BETTA** is what nightly I Dream
This Heavenly Letter says we can all **GET BETTA**
So Let's be a TEAM & **GET BETTA** 2GETHER!

GET BETTA BAA'BBIE!

I'M NOT AFRAID 2 DIE!

Dying is only the **Beginning** 4 You and Me
Because when you die you know who you're going 2 see
I refuse 2 be afraid of the *Thought of Death*
I'm going 2 live <u>Worry Free</u> until I take my last breath
And I'm willing 2 die 4 what I Believe In
Now I will do that 4 my Family and my True friends
Because GOD Delights in the death of one of his Precious Saints
Can you picture the picture I'm trying 2 Paint
It's going 2 happen 2 me and it's going to happen 2 you
<u>Dying is just something we all have 2 do</u>
My Appointment, my Time no one but the Farther knows
Now that's just how this *Life was Designed 2 Go*
When death comes Knocking at your Door
It doesn't matter if your 2, 3 or 94
Dirty rich or Filthy poor
If it's your time you might as well answer <u>Destines Door</u>
Now death is nothing 2 be afraid of
Because in death GOD is still showing his ***Unwavering Love***
So undercover brother there's no need 2 run and hide 4 cover
Death is something we have no control over
Death is coming no matter who you are
You're not exempt just because you are a <u>Famous Movie Star</u>
I know where I'm going when I leave from here
That's why ya boy has Absolutely nothing 2 fear
And I hope what I said came across Crystal Clear
Forget you death you ain't scaring nobody here!

52

Heaven

Heaven to me, is on the other side
That's where your love one is, you know the one that died
Heaven is the place where you go to get some Rest
Because you came to **Earth** and you gave it your Best
Heaven is your Reward for a job Well Done
Because you came, <u>You Conquered</u> and now you're gone
Heaven is a place where there's nothing but **Majestic Light**
Not like down here where you have day and night
Hell is wrong and **Heaven** is Right
It's a place where no one has to <u>fuss and fight</u>
About <u>who's wrong and who's right</u>
Heaven is your **True Home** can't you see
Heaven is the place where *Everyone Wants To Be*
It's definitely the place <u>I Want To Go</u>
Because it's a place, where no one has to be poor
Hey, we can have **Heaven** right here on **Earth**
<u>However, We Must Come Together First(1ST)</u>
Now that's something that would make GODS Heart Burst
Because <u>UNITY</u> is what he Thirst
See, <u>WE</u> bring **Heaven** down by *(Coming Together)*
Heaven told me to tell you, <u>"That's the Only Way Things are Going to Get Better"</u>
Heaven came into my Heart in this <u>Heavenly Letter</u>
Heaven told me to tell you one more time <u>It's About To Get Better!</u>

Conversation with Dr Martin Luther King

Dr. King can we conversate for a spell?
I need 2 know how we as a people can finally gel?
Because division has us visiting an early hell
Dr. King I just wanted 2 let you know
You're the reason I continue 2 strive and continue 2 go
Because what you done was a Tremendous Thing
You gave a lot of Good People a Good reason 2 Sing
I can hardly wait 2 hear those Freedom bells when they BEGIN 2 Ring
I Thank GOD 4 using you 2 pave the way
It was a sad day when you exited the Broadway play
I read a lot about what you had 2 say
You preached UNITY was the only way
Uniting the Souls is what I'm trying 2 do
Would you ask GOD 2 send his boy down a clue of what 2 do
Then he said 2 the Person of Self you must be True
And do what Leaders do
Which is do it Different do it New
Because you're of the Elite and the Few
He said you must understand you're here 2 Unite the human race
Because Humanity is stuck on 2nd base
GOD is about 2 put everything back in its proper place
Brace yourself because Truth and Reality are about 2 hit you in your face
Because a Piece of Heaven is what Togetherness makes
So Unite All Do whatever it takes
Remember GOD has the power 2 make earthquakes shake
The True Revealer *and Exposer of the fake*
Dr. King what if I get scared and frighten along the way
He said When you do that's the time you Need 2 pray
Then all fear will go away
Dr. King man why did you have 2 die?
I find myself asking that question why
Then he said GOD has his reason
Remember every man has his appointed season
It's just your time to Carry the Torch
So go get the Living off Life's Porch
Tell them 2 Get in the Game
If they don't want things 2 remain the same

Dr. King how do I get the ears 2 listen?
So I can tell them all the wonderful things they're missing
Just speak what GOD has told you 2 say
In the <u>Beds of Truth</u> *is where you NOW lay*
So let the Tongue Spit her Spray
Dr. King <u>Can I have all the answers 2 life's Test?</u>
He said you must understand when GOD sent you he <u>Sent his Best</u>
With that said maybe you can give your nerves some Rest
Believe me you have nothing 2 fear
<u>Just let the Holy Spirit Guide and Steer</u>
Then what you say will cause the <u>Inhabitants 2 Cheer</u>
Dr. King Do you have a Message 4 the People?
He said tell them they must <u>Become a People</u>
<u>Become a People</u> *is what the Good Dr. Said*
Hurry hurry b4 innocent people are dead
He said remember <u>Until All are Free None are Free</u>
<u>The I must become a WE</u>
<u>Forming the Most Perfect Tree</u>
That Great Tree of Life
So now you have all answers 2 the Issues and Problems of Life
<u>Simply Come Together</u> *for the Better*
The whole world needs to listen and read this letter
<u>LOVE and UNITY</u> *is the only Message you Need 2 Preach*
With GOD on your side nothing is out your reach
Hate and division has been faded with much bleach
Sit back because <u>GOD the HEAD TEACHER is</u> *about 2 TEACH*
Dr. King one more thing before you have 2 go
I just want 2 Thank you <u>4 Opening up Opportunities Door</u>
Now <u>We as a People</u> *can finally Soar*
Dr. King I too have a Dream
<u>My Dreams</u> *is that* <u>Your Dream</u> *would no longer be a Dream*
<u>Chosen King</u> *was Dr. Martin Luther King*
Who said <u>Uniting Every Living Thing</u>
Should be your Only Thing
So hold Heaven down Dr. King
Until <u>WE LET TRUE FREEDOM,TRUE FREEDOM RING</u>
And this WAS <u>My Conversation with Dr. Martin Luther King</u>
<u>Who had a GREAT DREAM</u>
<u>That the Whole World would become 1 PERFECT TEAM!</u>

The GIFT!

I Stir up **The Gift** within me
So the <u>Whole World</u> can see
I'm the Present under the Christmas Tree
Because the **Gifted One** is who I be
The Gift has me b4 Great & Mighty Men
The Gift that overpowers sin
I've been ***Blessed on Every Hand***
With **The Gift 2 Understand**
Most Gifted in the Land
Blessing Every Woman & Every Man
The Gift of Healing Sounds so Appealing
Use Me GOD because I'm Ready & Willing
The Gift gives me that Extra Kick
O Might Gift of Mine Help the wounded, Help the sick
I Thank GOD 4 this ***Most Precious Gift***
<u>2 Edify Motivate & Uplift</u>
The Gift was in me from the onset
It's when Love & I met
The Gift I have is **The Gift of Love**
I received it from GOD Above
The Gift is available 2 all
On its Mercy you need 2 call
If you're stuck on stall
<u>I Got LOVE</u> so how can I fall?
Feast & Feed on what you need
I Panted LOVE in your Hearts which is the Perfect seed!

Out the Blue

I'm coming Out the Blue in Open View
Before your Eyes is how the Best are Grew
You can call me <u>The Attention Getter</u>
Only the haters will be bitter
It's like I Magically Appeared
I'm to be Embraced and not feared
I know I Manifested so quickly
I'm Healing for the sickly
I've hatched like a newborn chick
My Words gave the world a much-needed kick
Out the Blue came the Truth
It came from the broadcast booth
It made the tight loose
It brought Healing for the Abuse
It saw its shadow like the ground hog
It sounds more like a Roaring Lion than a barking dog
Out the Blue, Out the Blue, Out the Blue
Something New is Coming at You
If you have Eyes to See
You can see Heaven coming out of me
AS MY words begin to Manifest
Because I'm Blessed to be the Best
Because I've been looming around my Creator
So I can be able to Man Handle you haters
Can't you tell, I got that brand new car smell
I'm coming Out the Blue is what I yell
Like a bat out of Heaven not Like a bat out of hell
Out the sky is where my Words fell

So get use to this Out the Blue stuff
Just let me know when you had enough
Because I'm sturdy like those twins Rough and Tough
I'm defending the Kingdom like Luke Sky Walker
When I get through, you'll know I'm GODS #1Talker
Tha Truth has Nasty Knots to untie
Because the Creator has heard our cry
Behold my Eyes have Seen The Light
Out the Blue GOD made Everything Alright!
The Unknown has become the Known
From all the Prayer Seeds that have been sown
Truth has Top Authority
And it was given to GODS #1 Minority
Like a 4 way stop sign I'm going in All Directions
Like a Hall of Mirrors I'm giving off all kinds of
Reflections
Like toast the Truth has popped out
Like dandelions I've began to sprout
Because Out the Blue I came
And LIFE will never again be the same
I'm Out the Blue I must Confess
So LOVE me for my Newness!

Unexpected Blessings

Unexpected Blessings are Coming my way
They came from people I didn't know is all I'm trying 2 say
It energized me like the Pink Energizer Bunny
It came in the color of that **Green Stuff** called **Money**
You never know where your help is going to come from
Be it a Stranger, be it a Bum
GOD gave me sum enough 2 even *Bless my Mom*
Unexpected Blessings can really make you <u>Believe in GOD</u>
When it comes it makes you feel strange & odd
Hey that's just the Creator doing His job
Those **Beautiful Blessings** caught me by surprise
What they done brought tears 2 my eyes
Unexpected Blessings always come in a ***Nick of Time***
Just when I'm down 2 my last dime
Something Good happens Every Time
Unexpected but Expected because *I Prayed*
I'm standing on the <u>Promises of GOD</u> that he already made
Expect the unexpected when you're feeling Dejected
A Great Future 4 us all is 2 be Expected
That's what my Senses just Detected
I got Unexpected Blessings is what I'm Confessing!

THE FUTURE

The Future belongs 2 the Living
We won't make it if the people don't <u>Start Giving</u>
GOD gave that which is 2 come 2 us
That's why Teaching our Children is a must
In GOD is who we need 2 Trust
The Future only frightens those who prefer Living in the dead past
In **The Future** there will be no guns 2 blast
Because firearms will be done away with
With no bodies 2 hit
Because with GOD is where we're going 2 sit
Thanks GOD 4 the Revelations I so often *Spiritually Spit*
The Creator has placed Eternity in our hands
It's not in can't but <u>CANS</u>
The Future was implanted in our Heart
That's where <u>The Potter </u>placed it at the start
It's just our time 2 do our part
The Future is about <u>Love & Undividable Unity</u>
The True Community filled with *Joy & Beauty*
It will be a Wonderful sight 2 see
Now that's how **The Future** looks 2 me
A Future where all people <u>Live Comfortable & Free</u>
That's **The Future** 4 Sure
Because **LOVE** WAS & IS the Cure
Because **LOVE** makes All things Pure
So get ready 4 the immediate Future
We can Write our own Script & Choose our own Course
The Future will work itself out So **REJOICE!**

Make It Happen

Refrain from saying the unkind and negative thing
Just think of the pain it would bring
Why not be the one that makes a person want to sing
Keep the promises that you make
No matter what it takes
Live real and not fake
Apologize for your mistakes
<u>Make It Happen</u> is the Word of the Day
I'm making things happen, so get out the way
Love your family members while you can
Lets Unite and hold each other's hand
Come on people it's time to take our last stand
Because I'm Dreaming of the Promised Land
In the Venues of Love is where I dwell
<u>Make It Happen</u> is what I began to yell
And I'm moving faster than a turtle or a snail
Be the Good that you desire to see
Pray that the Lord Most High would set us all free
Making things happen grows the Perfect Tree
So <u>Make It Happen</u> because there's no time for nappin
I did something is the reason Heaven's clappin
With my foot tappin and never before heard rappin
Sit back and Watch me <u>Make It Happen!</u>

We Need Change

We Need Change in every neighborhood
From Civic Park to Cottonwood
I mean a **Change** for everyone's good
We Need Change that's going to even the playing field
Because it's time for all this racism and discrimination to yield
Because we have new gardens to till
We Need Change and I don't mean any harm
But baby, it's time to sound the panic alarm
And this ain't coming from Jimmy Crack Corn
Nor will I be condemned or scorned
We Need Change in our schools
Because from what I see they think we're nothing but lowly fools
Because they refuse to give our children their proper tools
And GOD can talk through me if he talked through mules
Wake up slavery is still in our mist
And I tell you it has me pissed
Change is the Greatest Twist
At it the Devil pumps his fist
We Need Change in our American Government
And the **change** isn't in Superman or Clark Kent
If you get what I meant
We Need Change before it's too late
Dressing up in Love and taking off the hate
And this is something that just can't wait
I need your help like Adam needed Eve as a helpmate
We Need Change to come **Change** the way things are
Because what we've been doing hasn't gotten us very far
So **Change** will you come and **Change** the game
Will you send division back from which it came
We Need Change and the **Change** that's going to be
Most definitely is going to start with me!

What's Your Purpose?

What's Your Purpose for being here on planet earth?
What's the reason for your Timely and *Miraculous Birth*?
Everyone who breathes has a chance to Achieve
All that person has to do is Believe
All human beings were sent here with their own GOD sent **Mission**
Could this be the reason for so many different religions?
It seems as if everyone knows his or her **Purpose** but misled us
It's like we as a people somehow missed the **Purpose Bus**
We need to stop feeling sorry for ourselves and dry our misty eyes
Then maybe we'll begin to see through the deceit and horrible lies
Your Purpose is something you plan or intend to do
Yes, sleepy head I'm talking to you
Something in my heart tells me, "We're suppose to Help and be there for
one another"
Because the Good Book tells me, "You're suppose to be my Spiritual Sister
and Spiritual Brother"
Mother Nature fits all her children with something to do
Because there's something, a Job only you can do
Finding Your Purpose is not up to me but it's up to the Person called
(YOU)
Now **GOD'S Purpose** is to **Nurture, Comfort** and **Love You**, for (YOU)!

Live In Me

Live in me, live in me, live in me
Come on GOD would you live in me
It's me, asking you to **Live In Me**
Let my ears hear and my eyes see
LORD be the blood in my body that doesn't bleed
<u>Plant your Spirit In Me</u> like a harvesting seed
Without you there can be no me
Like a good parent O'LORD help me be
Like bifocals help me see
And let the whole world know you **Live In Me**
LORD let your Anointing begin to fall
Like the people of Jericho knock down my walls
Talk to me like ya did the Apostle Paul
Give me the Strength for the long haul
I've reserved a place for you to reside
If I tell the people to seek you will you promise not to hide?
As Your SPIRIT **Beautifies my Soul**
That Invisible Helper makes me complete, it makes me whole
GOD be the wings that helps me Glide
Like the New England Patriots let me be on the ***Winning Side***
Come on GOD let me see you Heal
Give me that <u>Satisfaction Guaranteed</u> Tattoo and Seal
HOLY SPIRIT I'm hoping to be your #1 pick
I hate devils because they're low down dirty tricks
Stiff pricks, jungle bunnies and country hicks
Let my body be your dwelling place
Through me LORD fight the people's case
Like baseball move me over to the next base

You living in me is what I chase
Let it be seen all over my face
Give me the Spirit that gives me LIFE
Live In Me and forgive me for asking you twice
Live in me, live in me, live in me
Come on GOD would you live in me
I need you Deeply Implanted in my heart
Because that makes me Protected and that makes me Smart
Change me like Superman did Clark Kent
For my wrongs let me quickly repent
With you on my team how can I lose?
That Great, Good, Gracious Spirit is what I choose
Live In Me Spirit is what I shout
Because I know you have something to talk about
Give me that Extra Strength and that Extra Clout
Live In Me like an inserted computer disc
I got FAITH so I'm taking an Everlasting risk
I need you O'LORD to order my <u>Every Footstep</u>
It's me Jimmy Lee screaming for your Help
Lead me from over here to over there
Let the Whole World begin to Graciously Share
I'm hollering out to the GOD of the Sky
For my piece of the Spiritual Pie
<u>Unconditional Love</u> is what I'm looking for
As I make my request for more
You have blessed me with **Extraordinary Speed**
You're my Owner because you have the Deed
Love me so I can LOVE others
Spread your SPIRIT to all my brothers and sisters
We need you to oil and anoint our achy joints

Like Basketball Star A I score the most points
But I throw assist like The Lakers Magic
Without you life would be tragic
So make your way, my way
Like air you're here to stay
Live In Me so I can live
Because I Love the Power that Love gives
Give me the <u>Freedom to be Free</u>
Let loose the shackles that have a hold on me
Like a Prime Time lawyer I present my case
I want to meet Freedom face to face
I just want to know how she taste
O'LORD let not my LIFE be a waste
You living in me is my Chief Aim
Let these WORDS reach the <u>Author</u> of this here game
Live In Me so I can bring you worldwide Glory and Fame
After all isn't that the reason that I came
Thanks GOD for living in me
Look out for me, as you feed me and clothe me
To the GOD living in me I get on my knees
Asking you to **Live in Me** Please
To the GOD I thought was a he but turned out to be a SHE
The One who Trusted me enough to **Live In Me!**

I AM

I AM is who I AM
GODS Perfect Lamb
More Powerful than Uncle Sam
I AM Great
Because one day I will be Head of State
If you don't Believe I tell ya just wait
The Great Creator has already sealed my Fate
I AM a Dreamer
Because I get the dirt out like a Stanley Steamer
And Jesus is the Perfect Redeemer
I AM Renowned
Because GOD told me what's going down
And I'm Funnier than the funniest clown
I AM Real
Because I'm going 2 tell you how I feel
Yes GOD Blessed me with Many Talents & Many Skills
I AM Strong
Because I have the Power 2 right the wrong
And the Money Supply is longer than long
I AM Confident
Because I have the devils back pent
Powerless like a Cape less Clark Kent
I AM a Man
Because I'm not afraid 2 take a stand
Against those things I don't like and understand
I AM GOD'S Child
Hey what I'm doing makes Her PROUD
Which has my head in the clouds
And my conversation drives the ladies wild
I AM Complete
Because the devils butt has been beat
Burning in his own Hell of Heat
I AM a WINNER
Because GOD is my Center
On my I AMNESS take a chew
2 be continued because my I AM ain't through!

PATIENCE

All Good things come to those who wait
Just be sure you're fishing with the right bait
PATIENCE is nothing but Pure Inner Power
That's what it's going 2 take 2 climb the Highest tower
Practice *PATIENCE* when everyone around you is hurried and frantic
Because worry never solved anything so don't panic
Slow down, relax, read a GOOD BOOK
Do something constructive I don't know maybe you can cook
PATIENCE and **Diligence** like FAITH removes Mountains
Don't lose Hope keep on counting
Be Patient GOD is just using 2days difficulties 2 Strengthen you
Don't worry he's just equipping you 2 do what you do
But you say I want and need it Now
But Mother *PATIENCE* knows when and how
Therefore 2 being Patient I take my bow
As I milk life like a Prized Cow
So sit back and let *PATIENCE* do what *PATIENCE* do
Which **is Get You Ready** 4 what GOD has 4 you
Because GOD has a Gift waiting just 4 you
2 the Game of *PATIENCE* you must remain True
Because *PATIENCE* has me playing the waiting Game 2 just like you!

Where Is GOD?

Where is GOD, is the Question of the day?
Where are you GOD is what I pray?
Where do you stay, are you hiding in the horses hay?
I didn't find you yesterday but that's OK
I guess Hide and Seek is what you Love to play
Every ones looking up into the Big Blue Sky
Asking GOD Why, Why, Why?
People walking around with their noses all in the air
Because in their hearts, they really don't care
GOD when are you coming down from Heaven Above
To show your people some Heavenly Love?
The World is so Wicked can't you see?
Everybody Picking, Poking and Joking about me
God you and only you can set us Free?
Because our Glorious Savior is who you be
Where is GOD and does he/she really care?
I'm stuck 2 GOD like gum 2 hair
Behind the Curtains of Life is where GOD be
Manifest yourself so all can see
Lord, we need you to step down from your Majestic Throne
Before all your people are Dead and Gone
GOD you know is in your Soul
He isn't in Santa Clause because they say he lives in the North Pole
Finding GOD is my #1 goal
So watch out, because Devil Heads are about to roll
Lord, Move like you never moved before
And let us not ask, **Where is GOD** anymore
GOD is in every human heart
He has been there from the very start
I found GOD, which makes me very smart!

My Mind

Good Morning Oh Great Mind of mine
Which is a Gift from the Great Divine
So Mind it's time to Shine
Get my Life in order, get my life in Line
Because I Desire to be in GODS Perfect Will
I'm **a Genius** and that's for real
With the Anointing to Speak and the Anointing to Heal
Lord, keep me with the Youngest Body & the Youngest Face
Let **Wisdom, Knowledge**, and **Understanding** enter this place
Mind I need you to be my Ace
I need you to react with the Quickest Pace
The Mind of GOD is what I chase
Guide me to the Top of Every Mountain and Every Hill
Provide my Mind and Body with the Most Perfect Meal
Give me *Thoughts* that are Right
Give **my Eyes** the Most Perfect Sight
And let **my Tongue** shed Major Light
That brings much Delight
With **Ears** that listen with all their Might
So mind take my Thinking to New Heights
That flies Higher than the Windiest Kite
Be Cool, Calm, Collected and Under Control
7 and 11 when the Dices begin to Roll
Make my Life Complete and make my Life Whole
Shape me into the Most Beautiful Mold
Keep me Fresh and keep me Brand Spanking New!
On GODS Revelations is what I Wish to Chew
I Pray for Happiness in My Mind, Body, and Soul
Help me to Reach and Conquer Every Dream and Every Goal
Mind, I Command you to Perform at your Best
With the Answers to Every Test
So fill me with So Much Zeal and So Much Zest
And when I sleep give My Mind and Body the Most Perfect Rest
But most of all keep my Heart Pure
Make me Confident and make me Sure
I Desire to Think like GOD
Let it be Easy and not hard
Give me Perfect Balance in My Life
I'm asking GOD to be My Wife
A Creative Mind is what I got
Because I Talk to GOD A Lot
I have the Greatest Memory in the land

Because like All State Insurance I'm in GODS Hand
I Think Good therefore I receive Good
I DESIRE to be the Best because GOD said I could
Let My Mind Shine like the Sun
That's 2nd to None
I Win so I Won
Give me a Mind that Loves to have Fun
Because Perfectly is how my Mind is Spun
Thank you Lord for the Most Perfect Mind
The only 1 of its kind
The Solution is what My Mind Loves to Find
Because GOD my Mind belongs to you
I need a Mind that Rejects the false and Embraces the True
Best Mind <u>Ever</u> before We're through
Give me Infinite Intelligence from the Great Unknown
Put My Mind in that Perfect Zone
GOD I need you to be the Programmer of My Mind
With the Power to <u>Loose and Bind</u>
Let My Thinking be like the King of Kings
*And let **Our Words** Glide on Eagles Wings*
Give me the Power to Draw and Attract
Let My Mind Perfectly Add, Multiply, divide and subtract
Let My Mind Get Better every day
For a Mind and Heart like GOD is what I pray
So Mind would you lead me to my Maker?
Shake out Great Ideas like a Salt Shaker
GOD I offer up my Life and my Mind to you
That's all I know how to do
Because what I <u>Learned</u>, I <u>Learned</u> from you
Perfect Peace is what I'm pleading For
That's going to lead me to my More
I'm just asking for, a Mind that Loves to Soar
I Got My Mind on the Lord
Because the Universe and I are now on 1 Accord
And I'm hooked up to that Main Power Source
I Rejoice because Mother Nature is taking Her course
<u>Make Miracles happen Oh, Great Mind of Mine</u>
Let Signs and Wonders be the only Sign
Be Smarter like GOD the Father or GOD the Mother
Get in the Action, Mind because you're a Primetime Starter
Give me <u>Perfect Rhythm</u> and the Straightest Aim
And let me not get blinded by the <u>Quick Riches</u> and the <u>Instant Fame</u>!
With My Mind there's no limit to what We can do
<u>Because GOD no one has a BEAUTIFUL MIND like you!</u>

Thanks Women

__Thanks Women__ for leading the struggle, for leading the way
I'm sorry, what a hell of a price you had to pay
But you're Strong Tough TRIED & TRUE
I know Life's been beating you
__Miserably black__ and __Depressed blue__
Some of you __Women__ know I'm talking to you
But through it all GOD brought you through
I just want to Thank You for doing what you do
You've been GODS Foot Soldiers for way too long
I think it's time to dance and sing to a new song
You've been like the Early Settlers trying to pave the way
All this time no one has listened to what you had to say
But can I tell you today is your __LUCKY DAY__
Because the __Beautiful Woman__ didn't forget to pray
The flowers of your heart is about to Sprouty Sprout
Now that's a good reason to cry and shout
Tears of Joy is what I'm talking about
Come on Baabbie if you hear me, let me hear you shout
Girl you're so Sexy and you're so Fine
You're the reason the Sun Shines
The Woman is So Intelligent and so Very Smart
In __Thanking You__, I'm just doing my part
After all baby you stole my heart
In the womb of the woman is where all creation made it's start
I know you were beginning to wonder what's wrong
That's why you're always on the telephone
Between yourselves trying to figure out what's wrong
Because that brother you loved is long gone

Women, I know life hasn't been a cup of Lipton Ice-T
But what I bring to you is all Reality
<u>Hail to the woman</u> Praise her all down through history
Help Every Woman, Every Lady and Every Girl
Every Female Species in the World
You are Picture Perfect & the Definition of Beauty
I just wish you weren't so Dam moody
Look out because I got broken <u>Hearts to Heal</u>
Believe me I feel the pain that you feel
And I know it's Realer than Real
Because you have no time in the day to stand still
Like the High Jumper I'm here to <u>Raise the Bar</u>
I'm talking to you and you know who you are
I Love you ALL and that's For Real
And **Thanks** for all those hot Gourmet meals
Because the stomach never forgets, where its help comes from
You were so nice you always asked me, did I want some
You made me feel like **The King** is where I'm coming from
Here I come so get your breath mints or gum
Thanks for being such a <u>GOD sent Blessin</u>
And for all the Ironing and Midnight Pressin
Because without a doubt you're **GODS BEST**
I know you wouldn't have it any less
Hey, <u>GOD could be a Woman</u> I must Confess
Now I can rest now that I got that off my chest
Thanks, Rosa Parks for not getting to the back of the Bus
Because **The Beautiful Women** was made for all of us!

73

SMILE!

Is there a **Smiler** in the room?
Because your frowning is causing Gloom
Like the Legion of Doom
Anyway GOD Loves the way you **Smile**
It measures the Longest Mile
I'm laying **Smiles** like the carpenter who's putting down
Kitchen Tile
Because **Smiling** makes my Spirit howl
<u>By the looks of it, you haven't Smiled in a while</u>
A **Smile** is an Upward Curving of the Mouth
It goes North not South
A **Smile** is something the broken heart needs
The Mind is what it feeds
A **Smile** *is the cheapest way to Improve how you look*
Not in all those get Beautiful Books
The **Smile** you send out returns to you
The frowning you do makes me want to sue
Before the Victory comes the **Smile**
And you can't wipe it off with the Biggest Towel
Like a Victorious PRESIDENT I **Smile** in Style
And it drives the ladies wild
So do me a Favor and Bust the **Biggest Smile!**

My Life

This is **My life** at the age of 30
So forgive for my words being so wordy
But I'm at the laundry mat because my clothes are dirty
I'm pondering and asking GOD why
Does he like to see me cry?
Why does everything in life seem to be a lie?
Why did my grandma and best friend have to die?
So now debating with the **GOD of the Sky**
My very own <u>Spiritual Spy</u>
I'm missing my daughter because she seems so far away
Which makes my life dark and gray
Because I'm wishing I could give her a big hug and a kiss today
Because seeing her seems to make my day
Because I'm missing her more than I did yesterday
Bring us back together GOD is what I pray
In Life I've experienced my **Ups and Downs**
Some of the situations made my heart pound
As I fight my way to <u>Gain Economical Ground</u>
But the enemy was always trying to hold me down
So I began to write down how I felt
I wondered why life was whipping me with its belt
This is **My Life** on the real
So sit back as my heart begins to over spill
I grew up poor in the dirty south
Poverty always took food out my mouth
I'm talking so the pain can come out
So listen to my shout
Taking baths on the back porch is what we had to do
During the winter months we sholl went through
So Mr. Freeze I'm going to sue
Because what if that happened to you

What would you do?

The rats and roaches were live in roommates

The food was gone if you came home late

Lack and not enough seemed to be my fate

The <u>Wealth and Riches</u> would have to wait

Because we're still cooking dinners on the hot plate

As Vibe magazine voted us poorest in the state

My mom had us when she was only 14

And our house was a sore sight to be seen

But we tried to keep it clean

Neighborhood filled with weed smokers and dope fens

Neighborhood thief trying to sale 5 pairs of stolen jeans

Our house had holes in the roof and holes in the floor

Man we were poor

Not to mention a big 4x4 locking the back door

And some of us sleeping on the floor

And going hungry while living right behind the grocery store

This is My Life, My Life, My Life

The Blake St. Mad Butcher

I'm GLAD my past ain't got nothing on my Future

People stealing because of no food

We had to you silly dude

Because the store manager was mean and rude

And poverty is what we were trying to elude

We ate but it never seemed like enough

Man **4000 West Short 3**rd was more than rough

But it made me tough

As I dreamed of one day being the stuff

We had the raggliest house on the corner so I didn't want to be there

Because it was more than I could bare

Into my heart I'm giving you the deepest stare

I'm telling the Truth and I don't care

Kids making fun of the way my house looks

Because you wouldn't find are crib in no real estate book

So I'm on my own learning how to clean and cook
I'm the fisherman who has to bait his own hook
The meddling and teasing made me mad and sometimes sad
I also grow up without a dad
But I was the 1st **College Grad**
And this broke down house was all a brother had
But I dreamed of one day being glad
This house is torn down now but the memories last
This broke down house will always be a part of my past
Even without light, water or gas
With no lawn mower to mow the gas
Because momma's low on cash
And I'm hoping the summer would soon pass
Because these mosquitoes still biting me on my ass

This is My Life, My Life, My Life

The 1st **of the month** was the best time in this house
Especially if you were a rat or mouse
Cats and dogs taking food out my mouth
Now I got a frown going down south
We got these Wine O's coming all around
Acting like bad breath clowns
Drunk, stumbling and falling down
Now he's headed for the ground
As the children yell touchdown
Because someone just pulled his pants down
My Life will one day be a <u>Best Selling Story</u>
To GOD I give the Glory
Even though I sometimes got in a hurry
But he told me to relax and don't I worry
Because he was about to come through
With things that are new
Listen to ya boy Jimbo, and Roll with the flow

Because to the top is where I'm about to go
My New House is really nice
With no mice with hair lice
With an icebox that makes its own ice
To **My Life** GOD added spice
I was **Blessed Double** I was **Blessed Twice**
I'm so glad I took GODS advice
To be precise and GOD sholl knows how to entice
My Life has gotten Much Better
So finish reading this letter
Because **My New House** is well put together
With no rain drops coming in during bad weather
With furniture made from pure leather
Living like this it doesn't get any better
This is My Life, My Life, My Life
I'm laughing at poverty because oppression is what I beat
Success and Freedom is what I greet
Now I'm Wearing the best shoes on my weary feet
And I did it all and I didn't have to cheat
And my daughter is who GOD finally let me meet
Now <u>It's All –Good</u> the way it should
I got enough Money to build my own neighborhood
And my family and friends also have it Great and Good
The way I wished it always could
<u>Man it Feels Good to tell how you Truly Feel</u>
I want to Thank GOD for each and every meal
Every Talent and **Every Skill**, **Every Movie** and **Every Book Deal**
And for allowing me to conquer every mountain and every hill
MY LIFE is **Blessed** because I'm in <u>GODS Very Perfect Will</u>!

Let My People Go

Let My People Go is the Word from the LORD
Or here comes that Spiritual Extension cord
Let My People Go is what **Moses** said 2 Pharaoh
Bloody rivers is how his river began 2 flow
2 GOD you dare say NO
Let My People Go is what **Martin Luther King Jr** Loved 2 Preach
But the Dream was just out his reach
Lessons in history is what I'm about 2 teach
As the Prophet begins his speech
Let My People Go is what **Malcolm X** Voiced with the **Strongest Voice**
Come on people will you past this Spiritual Coarse?
He was hoping 4 a *Liberated divorce*
From their Economic Fever Blister
He had the Klan calling him Mr.
Let My People Go is what **Jimmy Lee** began 2 Rap
With things 2 entrap & power 2 zap
Giving the devil all he can handle
Putting his head on the trophy mantle
GOD said Let My People Go
You who love 2 keep people oppressed & poo
I can see the Freeman's Freedom Trail
Going 2 Heaven vacating hell
Getting back up because we fell
Thanks GOD 4 delivering us like **1**st **class mail**!

Don't Leave Us Behind

Don't Leave Us behind *2 face this all alone*
When you get there throw ya people a nice juicy bone
I know you're off playing Professional Footbull
But you can still give ya boy a call
You know we as a people are stuck on stall
You're like the Fall Guy because you're about 2 fall
I guess you forgot where you came from
You have Money but you're still dump
You're the Blackest Uncle Tom
Lowest Bum with the mustiest underarms
Don't Leave Us Behind *all we need is a Financial Push*
Come on your acting like stingy George Bush
And you know how hard it is on a brother
That's the problem we never help one another
And the distance is getting farther & farther
You've been dunked on by the New Vince Carter
You're a 5th *stringer & I'm a Starter*
And I'm not worried about being the next Martyr
Don't Leave Us Behind *you're all we got*
Like gravy & grits my Words are scaling Hot
Because a Helper of your own is what you're not
Happiness comes from helping others
This is 2 all my Wealthy Brothers & Sisters
Pull us up 2 & stay True
Because Life is beating your people Confused Black &
Oppressed Blue
Help Your race like other races do
Don't Leave Us Behind *2 flat line*
Come on man, because no one likes being left Behind!

Say NO to Drugs

Don't let drugs get you hooked
Or you'll be living like a bum the last time I looked
And it will have your mind handcuffed and booked
Drug prevention is the need of the hour
Because drugs steal your Natural power
Turning you into something that you're not
I remember when that brother use to have a lot
So leave drugs alone
Cut it off like a disconnected telephone
Bury it like a dog's bone
Say no to drug abuse
I'm squeezing on you like orange juice
You'll never start if you're smart
When you're shopping don't put it in your shopping cart
What the body doesn't know it doesn't miss
Please don't give drugs a kiss
Because drugs are our most powerful foe
With the sharpest arrow and bow
Don't be afraid to be yourself
Because it affects your breath, your wealth and your health
So don't do drugs little youngster
Because they might turn you into a mean old monster
Now people who do drugs are not all bad
They're just depressed, stressed, and sad
They just bit off more than they could chew
Now the drugs are taking them through
What if that happened to you?
What would you do?
Understand the drug user Please
Before you laugh or tease
Because their Addiction is a Major Disease
I'm just warning you of the affects
And that it will have your mind in a ship wreck
Down to your last paycheck
Peaking at you like Woody Woodpecker when he begins to peck
So find something new and productive to do
Because it's all up to you
So Stay in School and be Cool
And follow the Don't Do Drugs Rule!

81

4 The Children

Let these Poems **BLESS Every Boy** and **Every Girl**
Let them **Reach to the Ends of the World**
Let them Educate and Transform the mind
Let it get the Children in Line
Let Every Child get a Peek
Young Minds is what I Seek
Let the words KISS them on the Cheek
Keep me Humble keep me Meek
So Lord let me have the Children's Ear
Let your WORDS Guide and Steer
Give me the *Right Words* to Say
For a <u>Genius Mind</u> is what I Pray
Fill these POEMS with **Wisdom and Rhyme**
Let these Words detour US from a life of crime
<u>GOD I need your HELP</u>
Let these Words order OUR Every Step
Let the Information soak
MAKE them Laugh at all my/our jokes
Let me be more addictive than caffeine and coke
Let the World be **CHANGED** by them
Give me Every Her and Every Him
To myself let me be True
Let me be just like you
On GODS Vine is how I WISH to grow
Let these Poems pick us up if we're feeling low
And let these Words Change the way we Think
If our Thinking Stinks
Anoint Every Letter that's typed or written with lead or ink
The <u>Kid Master</u> is who I be
So Lord Gravitate all the Children to me
Let me be the one that Sets the World Free
Because Lord can't no one **LOVE** like *YOU & ME!*

Prayer for My Tongue

To the Great GOD of Speech
My Tongue is what I want you to Teach
Let it never get out your Reach
Let it Perfectly Speak and Preach
LORD I give My Tongue to you
So do what you do
Use it to Speak Things that are New
Let Every Word be Tried and True
Let My Tongue spread Truth
Put her in the broadcast booth
Keep My Tongue in line
Let me Speak what is Divine
With Words that Sparkle and Shine
LORD Help Me control what I say
Let me not talk out your way
Tongue games is what I love to play
Control Every Word is what I Pray
Keep her on display
You're the Molder and I'm the Clay
O' Great Tongue of Mine
Use Every Opportunity to Shine
Make sense when you Rhyme Every Time
Only blurt out what is Needed
Because the Heart is where the Good Stuffs been Seeded
You're loose and YOU can't be Impeded
I'm Talking 4 GOD now so I done Succeeded
So LORD let Your Tongue be My Tongue
Give me words for the old and for the young

Give me the most breath for my lungs
Let me know how the songs are suppose to be sung
For that Golden tongue is what I pray
Let the Gift of Gab come my way
With Lips of Mercy and A Tongue of Grace
That stares Truth Directly in the face
Use <u>My Tongue</u> to deliver and heal
Give <u>My Tongue</u> the most skills
That's able to Amaze and Thrill
And revive those who are ill
Let <u>My Tongue</u> be Truthful when <u>My Heart</u> begins to Spill
To the Tongues Power I take my kneel
It's all YOU LORD that's the Deal
Let Every Word be what you would have Said
Let <u>My Tongue</u> be able to raise the Mentally Dead
With you GOD I THEE WED
Because <u>My Tongue</u> is controlled by the True GOD HE

I'M LOST

I don't know where I'm going
I Got Lost when it started snowing
I've somehow lost my way
2 find myself is what I pray
I can't seem 2 read the signs
Which one of these roads is mine?
And GOD says, Whichever one you take will be fine
GOD Loves the man who's not afraid 2 explore
I'M LOST but GOD has something in store
I had 2 travel alone
Passing through life like a Kidney Stone
I screamed until the pain was gone
I Got Lost trying to figure out
What life was all about
So now I no longer doubt
As I begin 2 Bud and Sprout
Adversity got me built and stout
With a hellva a lot of things 2 shout about
I was lost and JESUS is who I found
Which turned the world upside down
I GOT LOST 2 pay the cost 2 be the BOSS
I found GOD so I'm thankful 4 no longer being lost!

Mother's Day

Mother's Day is all about **Mother's** and **Moms**
From **Mother's** is where all Creation comes from
Nothing and no one Loves like a <u>Devoted</u> **Mother**
My <u>Appreciation</u> for you is something I can no longer hide or smother
<u>Mother's are the Greatest Females of them All</u>
When in trouble I know who 2 call
A ***Mother's Love*** is not easy 2 explain
Thanks 4 Enduring those long labor pains
Mother's Day should be **365 days** a year
<u>I Love you</u> Mom is what I want you 2 hear
You held me so close, you held me so near
Your ***Warm Embrace*** squeezed out all my fears
When I had a problem you were all Ears
Thinking how much you Love me almost brings me 2 Tears
Mother's Day is my gift back to you
Just so I can **Thank You in Open View** for all you do
Every Trait Every Talent that I got I got from you
<u>I Love you</u> and don't let that take you by Surprise
Mother's are like the **Morning Sun** there's no doubt that they will rise
I'm from you is the reason we have the same color eyes
Thinking about you Girl How Time Flies
<u>I Pray for all the Mother's of the World</u>
The ones that use 2 be Little Girls
Because without you there could be no me
My Love 4 the Mothers is what I want all Yal 2 see!

Mother's

Mother's bring **Joy** & **Delight** to my Soul
Praising these Women is my Goal
So I Shout **Thanks** *Mother's* for <u>Giving US Life</u>
If you were a pie you'd be the Perfect Slice
So I pray that life would treat you *Extra Nice*
Mother I came from the Womb of your Belly
You Loved me even when I was stinky & smelly
<u>For 9 months</u> you became my House
Like a kangaroo Pouch
Thank Goodness you didn't kick me out
You loved me without condition
You're the **Best Mom** is what I had to mention
Slaving COOKING Great meals in the kitchen
Hey Mom you deserve the Royal treatment
And no amount of money can afford the payment
Mother's Thanks for being an <u>Extension of GOD</u>
You stayed True even when things got hard
I Love you Mommy from the <u>Bottom of my Heart</u>
That's why *Mother's* are at the top of every Billboard and Chart
Thanks Mommy 4 doing your Part
All I can say is <u>THANKS</u>
Because Number #1 is how all *Mother's* are Ranked!

My Culture Was Taken from Me

My Culture was taken from me
Like an uprooted Oak Tree
1 & 2 are present but someone swiped 3
So now I'm a car without a key
Someone took **My Culture** & I'm looking 4 it
Watch out cause I'm about 2 throw a hot African fit
The bull's eye is what I'm about 2 hit
Let the Light of **My Culture** be lit
I screaming because I want it back
I need it like Jill needed Jack
Its shell is what I'm about 2 crack
Not knowing gets hard 2 bare
Get me there & pay the travel fare
Does anyone have a **Culture** they could spare?
Speak up if you truly care
I don't know me is the reason 4 the blank stare
My Culture is calling out my name
Not knowing has cost us so much shame
Explain 2 me the name of this identity theft Game
Tell me who I do I blame?
My Culture was taken from me without my permission
In **My Culture** is my God Sent Mission
I don't know what 2 believe is it Fact or Fiction?
They kidnapped our **Culture** from us
So don't be telling me 2 hush
Because in **My Culture** is that **Golden Key**
That's sure 2 **Set us Free!**

OWN MY OWN

OWN MY OWN in this big bad place
Doing my best 2 keep pace
And remain among the human race
The Truth is what I began 2 chase
As I slide safely in2 2nd base
Death always cause the eyes 2 cry
As I give the Game of Life a try
Sitting in my car listening 2 the sounds of the night
As the economic mosquitoes begin 2 bite
ON MY OWN 2 find out what's wrong and what's right
As Mother Truth begins 2 shed Her Light
Because Adversity trying 2 zap my might
ON MY OWN so I'm all by myself
Last one left dusty because I been on the shelf
Serving more than one of Santa's Elf's
In my search 4 GOD and Material Wealth
Hold up I'm tired let me catch my breath
Because it takes so much energy trying 2 find your True Self
In the woods listening 2 those nightly sounds
Because sometimes you just don't want 2 be found
Because people like keeping you bound
ON MY OWN since the age of 10
O if I could tell you the places I've been
While life still kicks me in my Spiritual shins
Religion revealing all my sins
ON MY OWN 4 one reason
So GOD could simmer and season
ON MY OWN which means I'm all alone
2 cry and moan getting grown
GODS very own clone
Hey what I Learned I Learned ON MY OWN!

Win!

I will do those things in which it takes to WIN
With the Perfect out come in the end
So Lord give me the will POWER to WIN
Give me a Perfect Score I mean a Perfect 10
So Lady Luck would you mysteriously come my way
In the House of Winners is where I want to stay
I'm a Winner is what I loudly and proudly shout
So Lord give me Super Confidence and Major Clout
Because I really Expect to Dominate and WIN
Every Competition, every race, every throw and every spin
A Winning Mentality is my Tattooed Reality
Keep me from all loses and calamity
So Great Spirit release those profound prophetic secrets
I'm a Winner so all I produce is #1 hits
You told all I had to do was speak it
Like a snitch leak it, I mean release it
Show Me How to Win, Show Me How to Win
Show me, Show Me, Show Me LORD How to Win
Take me LORD to the Pinnacle of Success
Because I'm Blessed to be the Best
Championships Trophies and rings is all I want to see
Hear me if your favorite is who I be
Like Jesus I got that Winners look
Like Wilt Chamberlin I've be Placed in the Records book
Thanks Hook Master for the Perfect Hook
I WIN because I do what it take & did what it took
The rector scale says my Words is the reason the earth shook
WHY I WIN is a Best Selling Book

I got Beautified Beauty and Gorgeous Grace
Let it be seen all over my face
The Victory cake is what I wish to taste
Let not one minute of my life be a waste
The Winner's Circle is what I DESIRE to be in
I'm a Winner and Winners always WIN
Show Me How to Win, Show Me How to Win
Show Me, Show Me, Show Me LORD How to Win
So let me do what Winners do
Just allow me GOD to stay close to you
I believe I can WIN and that's True
Because my GOD designed me a lit bit better than you
I have that Winning blood running through my veins
With Perfect Perfection let me Perfectly Train
Lord, just help me do my part
Make me intelligent and very smart
Give me the Upper Hand GOD because I have your ear
Let me Get Better Day-by-Day and Year-by-Year
On the Winning side is where I be
So Lord, put that Winning Spirit in me
1st place is all I want to see
It all sounds good to me
Show me how to win GOD My closes Friend
I'm a Winner is the message I'm trying to send
On GODS Team is where I be
And I can be Who ever I wish to be
Which is the Very Gifted Jimmy Lee!

Baby Momma Drama

Baby Momma Drama is the horror story I'm here to tell
So all Baby Mommas can go booty butt- naked to hell
Because your hater smell is leaving a nasty trail
Baby Mommas are the Devil is what I began to yell
As they anticipate child support checks coming in the mail
All depressed because you're no longer bony or frail
You were pregnant 9 years ago but your stomach has yet to go down
You money hungry money hound
You're the reason for those screaming sounds
Baby Mommas are the #1 sellouts of the year
Go away Baby Mommas, you're not wanted here
You're the reason Baby Daddy guzzling down 30 packs of beer
Under cover Devils is what the Little League Cheerleaders began to cheer
Got Baby Daddies jumping from the highest peer
Because you taking all his money is his only fear
Baby Mommas are the ugliest things walking the earth
Your own Momma tried to push you back in at birth
Because she was a Baby Momma 1st
Watch out, because King Baby Daddy has bubble bath water to splash
And to tell you to get your mind off my cash
As I put a lock on your pocket book called the purse
You're on child support so reverse
I hate Baby Mommas so bad I didn't have to rehearse
You're the reason I started back to cuss
So shut up because it's my time to fuss
Because I can't have you and the government coming against us
I'm here to reveal who you really are
You burnt out shooting star
You look like a overweight monkey hanging from a rusty monkey bar
You're not who you appear to be
You fake tree, that was your last shopping spree
You're a woman but you look like a retarded he
You eat more coochie than me
Baby Mommas are women with very low self-esteem
So forgive me for letting off some much needed steam
Because Baby Mommas are nightmares instead of dreams

As they melt like spoiled ice cream
Because when it comes to Baby Daddies, I'm the Dean
And why is your dookie always dark green
Looking like an out of dope, dope feen
Because all you do, is lie and scheme
Dressed up like a broke Aunt Ester and the Bald head Mr. Clean
BABY MOMMA DRAMA
I'm kicking all Baby Mommas off the team
Because you're meaner than Mean Joe Green
So I'm putting you on high beam
And telling you to take off those too tight jeans
Baby Mommas must never be trusted
Watch out tricks because you've been busted
Because money and Big Daddy Pipe is what you lusted
I heard you ran into one that rusted
You need to get your mind dusted and attitude adjusted
Because you smell like a old Musty White Boy, who lost his convoy
You takers of all of Baby Daddies joy
Because you love to annoy
So I'm throwing you away like an old raggedy toy
And treating you like drunk Elroy
And making you grow a beard like Pastor Troy
Because when it comes to women, you're a diseased decoy
You're a hater by trade
When I get through you're going to need a Band-Aid
This is a Baby Mommas raid
Because from the evil dust is how you were made
Always trying to get paid
Tasting like sugarless Kool-aide
Make me hate I ever meet your crazy, lazy, driving Ms Daisy looking ass
You didn't gas up, so you're out of gas
When it comes to Baby Daddies, ya'll done messed with your last
Because getting you off my back is my only task
So Monster you can take off the Monster Mask
So Baby Mommas who looks bad now
With your 1 eyebrow
You stinky, diseased, plagued, MADD, cow
You even tried to get little Bow Wow

To King Baby Daddy take your bow
On your dam knees is how
As I spoon-feed you Generic Puppy Chow
And ask for forgiveness, and stay your ass out my business
As I wipe your filthy ass all across the dirty floor
All sprung because I made that coochie sore
I'm rejecting you like the voters did Al Gore
I'm uprooting you by the core
And shutting down your favorite store
Anyway, when I met you, you were poor
And don't make me call you a whore
BABY MOMMA DRAMA
Baby Mommas are half-human and half retarded horse
One day of marriage and he wanted a divorce
Because you're a Engineless Pinto pretending to be a Rolls Royce
Watch out, because Father Nature is about to take his course
So Confused Nothings listen to my Angelic Voice
Baby Mommas you've lost all your power
So get jobs paying more than $6.00 an hour
I tasted your coochie and it tasted sour
You're a withered flower, a crumbling tower
Take a bath instead of a shower
Baby Mommas produce goat milk from their tits
Eating low fat Kibbles & Bits
Giving Baby Daddy fits, causing worry zits
Having kids just to try to keep a man, but he still ran
Instead of sexing you, I prefer over using my hand
Mirror, Mirror on the wall who's the worst looking in the land
It's the Baby Momma that transformed into a man
Who is caught in the quick sand
Who's seeking counseling from panties wearing Peter Pan
Baby Mommas look like the bottom of my shoe
And I just intentionally stepped in some Dog and Sick Baby Doo-Doo
I know you've been practicing Voodoo
By the way, I saw your look alike at the zoo
And IT said, "---- you too"
Baby Momma Destroyer is my main tattoo
666 is the unlucky # you just drew

I'm closing your mouth with the most expensive Super Glue
My Mission is to talk about you in Open View
Because you're the fake and I'm the true
Like Muhammad Ali it's a 3rd Round Knock Out
This is how it feels to be talked about
Looking like the Lone Rangers lost scout
Baby Mommas are Walking Baldhead Vultures
Scavengers and pultures, creating their own cultures
But this time you've meet your match
I'm cooking your ass before you hatch
And throwing you away because you're a bad batch
Disease of the pocket is what you now catch
So you had better learn how to sew and patch
You're a pick pocketter who loves to snatch
Baby Mommas are all Mentally Retarded
Didn't say excuse me when she farted
The smell left when you departed
Eating all those beans is when the trouble started
You held it in which makes your breath tarted
Look out, Dummy you've been out witted and out smarted
Baby Mommas return to the Black Lagoon
And stop howling at the moon, you Erased Cartoon
You Crazy Loony Toon, you bent up fork and spoon
You're gone and not a moment too soon
Baby Mommas are the worst problem in every community
They Love division and hate Unity
So go back to your dark hole
And masturbate with the American flagpole
You animated troll and try to hide some of those stomach rolls
And stop cutting your man with those raccoon toes
And take off grandma's 1932 panty hoses
And get that dookie off your nose
The book of Baby Momma Drama has been Sealed and Closed
As they take an Everlasting Pose
Baby Mommas are put into Spiritual Commas
Because they are the Queens of Drama
Sorry I had to eat ya'll ass alive with sauce from Tony Roma's
But I had to put an end to my Bad Baby Momma Drama!

Can I be Real?

Can I be real Can I tell you how I truly feel?
On being real who's going to foot the bill?
Hcy on being Real
You're faker than the Game show Let's Make a Deal
We're like puppets hanging from strings
The Truth is the only song I'm going to sing
No one is willing to be real
So life is stuck on stand still
Like the gravedigger I got holes to fill
Because you're more confused than Jack and Jill
Who fell Helplessly down the hill
What if I decide to be myself?
And take the Book of Realness off the shelf
They say a Realest never accumulated much wealth
But fakeness is bad on your health
So I can no longer hold the Truth up under my breath
I'm the Whistle Blower so you can call me the Ref
Hollywood want- a -bees wearing fake fur
Not sure if he wants to be a him or a her
Sorry Sir
Sit back as I take your minds on a worldwide detour
Because on being real you're not really sure
Should I stand my ground?
So the Truth can be found
Turn up the sound because fakeness is all around
In every town
I'm the Lifeguard and I won't let you drown
Cover up is the name on the game
The devil is the blame
Because what you do behind closed doors makes you shame
But I'm here to bring realness to the Hall of Fame
Can I be Real? Can I be Real?
Can I Tell you how I Truly Feel?

Bringing the real releases my pain
And that healing is the gain
Be real is what I told my brain
Grow Truth like the farmer grows grain
I got realness flowing through my veins
Because I'm hooked up to the real soul train
As the Universe lets loose the chains
Because I can no longer be contained
Should I be real, should I break the seal?
Or should I stand still, and take a chill pill?
And let the fakeness continue to rob and kill
As life goes around like a broke Farris wheel
I think it's time to be real
But before I do let me take a kneel
Because Prayer is stronger than Pennsylvania steel
And I'm not going to lie like President Bill
I'm ready to take the lie detector test
I'm butt necked so I'm undressed
Reality is what I'm here to deal with
From the heart the mouth will spit
In the Chair of Truth is where I sit
And this is no Hollywood Skit
This is real life my friend
That's the reason for my bloody shins
Look what happened to the Indians and red skins
It seems like another developing trend
Like Kuta Kenta I got to escape
I Guess I'll be the 1st to break the tape
I bake real like Grandma baking corn meal
Being real is in GODS Perfect Will
So let's make a deal to be real
Because it's the only way to get on GOD'S playing field
Should I be Real I done told you the deal?
I'm going to keep it REAL!

BUCKY BEAR

Bucky Bear the bear with **Black** *and* **Burgundy Hair**
He was Brave and not easy to Scare
This was a Bear too BIG to sit in your baby chair
When he walked by all the children would Look and Stare
Because they just saw a **Talking Bear**
Bucky Bear LOVES TO LAUGH
As he searches for food in the **Green Grass**
Because he had just gobbled up his last
But **Bucky Bear** found food <u>Right on Time</u>
When **Franky Frog** sold him a Meat sandwich for a Dime
Because he was his friend he threw in a **Fresh Lemon Lime**
Bucky Bear was Friends to All
Some were **Short and Small**
Some were **BIG and TALL**
Who Loved to play **Baseball**, **Basketball** and **Football**
When in trouble they would always give **Bucky Bear** a Call
Even though he slept through the winter and through the fall
Bucky Bear <u>LOVES to READ</u>
Because he knows that's what the Mind needs
Bucky Bear says *YOU CAN DO ANYTHING IF YOU BELIEVE*
Be Good and a **Big Bucky Bear Bear Hugs** is what you will Receive
GOD is the Head of **Bucky Bears** Life
No, **Bucky Bear** doesn't have a Bear Wife
But **Bucky Bear** will protect you from that Fake boogie man
He will always be there to hold your hand
Bucky Bear says *Always do your Best*

And be sure to **Study** for tomorrow's Big Test
Like superman **Bucky Bear** has a Capital **B** on his Chest
Bucky Bear says always remember to <u>Be Yourself</u>
And know your right hand from your left
Bucky Bear <u>Really Loves you</u>
Because that's what Good Friends are suppose to do
Now matter if your **Black** White **Red** or **Blue**
That's a Promise from **Bucky Bear** to Beautiful You
Bucky Bear has the <u>Biggest Heart </u>in the World
And says <u>Boys should Never Hit Girls</u>
Bucky Bear wants to give you a **Big Bucky Bear Bear hug**
As he rolls around on Mother's New Rug
Gazing at the **Lady Red Bug**
Who was also in search of a **Big Bucky Bear Bear Hug**
Bucky Bear <u>The Bear that really Care</u>
He throws his **LOVE** in the Air
And that's the story of <u>My Friend </u>**Bucky Bucky Bear**!

THE WICKED LIGHT IS PUT OUT!

It's time 4 the wicked 2 hit the road
Yes I'm kicking you out in the cold
Move you're not wanted here anymore
You're vacant like a closed down store
A lion that's lost its roar
A pimpless whore whose pantyhose are tore
You've been out done you stinky son of a gun
Your light is about 2 lose it shine
So go 2 the bench head 4 the pine
Because you've been caught in your own bind
The wicked light is put out can't you see
<u>He no longer holds the key</u>
Wake up and realize that you are free
His **Day of Judgment** is here
You devils have a right 2 fear
What was done in the dark has come 2 the light
As you vanish from the people's sight
You're not right so put your dukes up it's time 2 fight
The Victory has been won
Thanks 2 GOD'S only begotten Son
The wicked light is put out is what I shout
No longer able 2 sprout with no more clout
GLORY 2 GOD the wicked light is put out!

The Prayer Book

This is the **Wonderful Prayer Book**

My Prayers are simmering so it's Time 2 Cook

2 GOD is where all my problems were took

Because I'm in another episode with that devilish crook

I Thank GOD 4 <u>Anointing this Book of Mine</u>

Where **Prayers Grow** on the Wildest Vine

Because in this **Prayer Book** is where the Angels Wine & Dine

As I Read Line upon Line

Because the Words are **Beginning 2 Shine**

So Lord Give Ear 2 this Book of Request

We need you 2 come along 2 swat that pesky pest

As the Holy Ghost pounds on my Heart & Chest

Lord you Promised 2 hear me when I call

Let not these Words hit the Ground or Fall

Let this Prayer Book Bless Each & All

Every Answered Prayer is Heaven Sent

So B4 I Pray I better **Forgive all** & **Quickly Repent**

Because Prayer Time is Good Time Spent

HELP ME Lord because I have frustration 2 Vent

Up 2 Heaven is where my Prayers Went

So **Prayer Book** let these Words begin 2 Bleed

<u>Giving Every Reader the Assistance they Need</u>

As I Pray 2 be Totally Freed

Allowed 2 Thrive & Succeed

My Spirit is what I want you 2 Feed

Give our Spirit a Major Uplifting

Through your Word is what I been sifting

Looking 4 a way out

I Believe you **Answer Prayer** & that's No Doubt

So I Pray 4 the Words that are in this **Prayer Book**

I Prayed is the reason the Earth Shook

Because Prayer is the **Only Bait** you need on your Hook!

PRAYER 4 THE YOUTH

O' Great Shepherd of Heaven & Earth
Let me Pray 4 our Children 1st
4 their Safety is what I Thirst
I Pray 4 all the Youth of the World
4 all kinds of Boys & all kind of Girls
Send your Mighty Angels 2 their Aide
Protect Every Age & Every Grade
Let the violence begin 2 Fade
Make them Sweet like the Sweetest Kool-aide
O' Lord give the Youth something Productive 2 Do
Take away the old & Surprise us with the New
On Good Words let them Chew
Let them do what Children are suppose 2 Do
GOD Gravitate all the Children 2 You
Keep the Youth from things that cause serious Harm
Take the Youth O' Lord by the Arm
Fill them with Style & Charm
Be there 2 cover them while they go through their Storm
Teach the Youth what the need 2 be Taught
Every Boy & Every Girl needs 2 be Caught
Provide 4 their needs
Fill them with Good Deeds
My Prayer is that you will Help them Succeed
The Minds of Tomorrow is what I want you 2 Feed
Let the World be filled with Youth & Vigor
Get them in Shape so they can be Proud of their Figure
Let them Think B4 they pull the Trigger
Let us stop losing the Youth 2 the Early Grave Digger
Help the Youth Everywhere
Give them Parents that really Care
Educate their Minds in the Learning Chair
Thanks LORD 4 Helping the Youth
We all Love YOU & that's the TRUTH!

PRAYER 4 OUR SCHOOLS

2 the GOD who Guides the Human Heart
Let <u>Reformation in the Schools</u> Begin 2 Start
Fix what Discrimination & Division has torn apart
Get our Schools 2 the Top of the Charts
I Pray 4 ***School Safety & Protection***
Get the Right Board of Directors in Every Election
O' GOD let All Schools be **Properly Funded**
With the Quickness is how I Imagined You Responded
Our Schools need you in a Major Way
Hear the Children when they Pray
<u>Stop the Violence</u> that has so often Occurred
Let it be Rerouted & Detoured
Beautify Every Learning Institution
Give Us O'LORD the Solution
Lend Us your Mercy & Grace
Put a Big Smile on our Face
Let not our Youth Lives be a Big Waste
GOD will you get the School System in Line
Transform it like You Converted the Water into Wine
Give Us what we need in order 2 ***Successfully Succeed***
I'm following You LORD so Go Ahead & Take the LEAD
Give Every Child the Tools they Need
Because **Precious Minds** is what we have 2 FEED
LORD I Pray 4 Total Reform
Cover Us in Your Arms
Speak Eloquently 2 our Storm
Put Us in our Rightful Place
You made the Human Mind Our ACE
Come LORD 2 Fight our Case
Thanks 4 Bringing Us Out
<u>You're the BEST</u> without a Shadow of a Doubt
Help our Schools is what I'm Shouting About
Glory 2 GOD Glory 2 GOD is what I Loudly Shout
Thanks LORD 4 Getting Us Back on Track
Helping Us in the areas we have Lack
Equality 4 the White Equality 4 the Black
Because **When it comes 2 (Education we need 2 Lead the Pack!)**

PRAYER 4 EMPLOYMENT

LORD Good Work is what I Need
On your Promises is where I Feed
Let Every Application be a Growing Seed
Lead me 2 the Place where I'm going 2 Succeed
You know the Perfect Career 4 me
Make it Plain so I can Clearly See
Because GOD the Door Opener is who you be
So Properly Order my Feet
My Destiny is what I Pray 2 Meet
Put me in the Interviewers Seat
I'm Praying 4 something Positive & Productive 2 Do
My HOPE is that I could Work & Labor 4 You
When it comes 2 Bosses you're the True
I'll take White Collar or the Collar that turns Blue
I come 2 YOU
Because the Best Jobs come from You
So give me that Just Right Occupation
B4 you do let me give you a <u>Standing Ovation</u>
Because Praise brings you the Greatest Sensation
I'm Ready 4 my Graduation & Promotion
Thanks LORD 4 giving me Favor in Every Situation
And 4 giving me my Deepest Heart Desire
Help me out because I'm 4 HIRE
So LORD Set Me Free
<u>I want 2 Entertain & Use my Recreation Degree</u>
So let me Showcase my Talents & Skills
And let me Comfortably Pay all my Bills
2 Work 4 you LORD is what I Choose
The Position I Promise not 2 Abuse
With you as my Manger how can I Lose
So LORD Bless me because I've Paid my Dues
Thanks LORD 4 the Job I Got
And 4 Placing me in the <u>Most Blessed Spot!</u>

PRAYER 4 PURPOSE

2 the GOD of Heaven who Knows All & Sees All
4 my Purpose is the Reason that I Call
It's Me Roaming down the Hall
Is my Purpose short small large or tall?
Do I have 2 Scale another Wall?
Or Fall off my Horse like the Apostle Paul
I Pray 2 Know what 2 Be
Let the Vision become Clear 2 See
In my Dreams you can give me a Peek See
Because my Purpose Opens up my Life like a Master Key
I Pray 4 a Purpose that will bring you all the Glory
After All this is the Purpose 4 this Purpose Filled Story
My Purpose is 2 Get the Attention All on YOU
The GOD who is Tried & True
So the Finger Pointer is Pointing the Finger 2 YOU
Which is Something Brand New
Help Everyone Find out Why they are Here
Whisper our Purpose in our Ear
It's what our Heart wants 2 Know
Was I made 4 the Heat or 4 the Snow
Which Way Do I Go What Do I Do?
Will my days be Many or Will my days be Few
Just let me Accomplish what I'm Here 2 Do
Yum Yum I See the Birth of my Purpose Coming
It's the Reason I Started Humming
My Purposed has been Summoned
And it's so Uncommon
I have work that needs 2 be done
And it's Going 2 be Fun in the Sun
Get your Purpose because my Purpose Got Me
True 2 Myself is what I got 2 be
2 Yourself My Friend Always Be True
No Matter what you Do or Don't Do
Remember the Heart holds the Clue
Your Purpose is what You LOVE 2 Do the Most
Just Get the Help & Aid of the Holy Ghost
I Found My Purpose so I BOAST
SO 2 GOD I MAKE MY TOAST!
THANKS A LOT!

PRAYER 4 TRUTH

4 the **TRUTH** is what my Heart longs 4
Because I don't want 2 Live lies anymore
On the **Highest Levels** of **TRUTH** is where I Wish 2 Be
Place the **TRUTH** in my Face so I can Clearly see
Let my Heart be Discerning 2 what is Right
I know **TRUTH** is a Beautiful Sight
It's the **Perfect Light**
On the Flesh of **TRUTH** is what I Desire 2 Bite
As **TRUTH** sends falsehood 2 Flight
I want **TRUTH** like ring around the collar
I yearn 4 it more than that *Mighty Dollar*
I Pray 4 what I need 2 Know
TRUTH is what I want 2 Follow
Wind of **TRUTH** let me feel your Blow
Because I Love your *Distinguished Glow*
And the way you Cut High & the way you Slice Low
Let those *Truthful Bells Ring*
Because I like the way She Sings
Give me **TRUTH** because it makes Life Better
I Pray 4 All True's 2 Come Together
4 the **TRUTH** is what I Yell
Tell me Lord where has **TRUTH** fell
I'm digging 4 **TRUTH** like Bushes Oil Wells
Lies are like a Train that's Derailed
From the School of Life lies have been Expelled
Thanks Lord because **TRUTH** & I have Finally Gelled!

PRAYER AGAINST DEPRESSION

I come 2 you O' GOD with the Heaviest Heart
Asking you 2 Remove that Depressing Dart
Because the Hurt is tearing my Life Apart
I'm Depressed & I'm not making Decisions that are Smart
So I Need you 2 Clean My Heart
I Pray 2 be Released from this <u>Nasty Disease</u>
I'm on my Knees begging you Please
Put my Depression on Freeze
2 my situation I know you have the Keys
Let me not try 2 sleep my Life away
For the Solution is what I Pray
That will push my unhappiness out the way
So I can Cheerfully Play
Lord help me figure out the cause
Because I'm stuck on Pause
Hurry because Depression brings about the Early Death
<u>Discontinue the Pain</u> take it off the Shelf
Because the Depression is causing me bad Health
Freedom is what I yearn
As I do I Gigantic U Turn
In hell let my Depression Burn
Please LORD handle my *Top Concern*
The opposite of Depression is Happy
Because being Depressed makes us Feel Crappy
Being Happy makes me <u>Feel Good</u>
Chop down my sadness like Chopped Dead Wood
Thanks LORD 4 Releasing me from my Great Depression
I'm Delivered is my True Confession
It's in Recession a cut out Page & Section
The Loser in the Election
Not even coming in my Direction
Thanks GOD because that's the <u>End of my Depression!</u>

PRAYAER 4 DELIVERANCE

Deliver Me O' Lord in my distress
I'm wrinkled in Spirit so I need 2 be Ironed & Pressed
Deliver Me from being Down & Depressed
Turn my Midnight into a Miraculous Day
Because I Learned that Prayer does Pay
So do me a Favor & keep that Ugly devil at bay
Deliver Me from any Sickness or Disease
Bless me Lord Every Time I sneeze
Help Me avoid the traps that are laced with Cheese
You're so Gracious so I don't have 2 Beg & Plead
Your Assistance is what I desperately need
Take away the Strongholds which try 2 way me down
Give me away out when Life has me Chained & Bound
Let Sweet Victory be the only Sound
I need away 2 Escape
Where's my Superman Cape
Like curtains let your Anointing Drape
I Pray 4 Strength 4 every Battle
Protect Me like a Cattleman herds me like his Cattle
Keep me as I ride on the Saddles of Life
Deliver my Family, Friends, Husband or Wife
In the Safe Havens of your Arms is where I want 2 be
The Finish Line is what I want 2 See
They told me you Delivered & you did it 4 FREE
<u>RESUE ME</u> O' Lord in my *Time of Need*
As I Water my Prayer Seed
Be there 2 Heal every Scar that Bleeds
My HOPE is 2 be Totally Freed Indeed
I know you're a GOD who **Answers Prayers**
You're the number #1 Enemy Slayer
The Perfect Team Player
Deliver Me O' Lord if you Truly Care
Give us Justice Give us Liberty 4 our Adversity
Thanks Lord 4 Hearing my Plea!

PRAYER 4 COURAGE

O Great GOD of the Heavens Above
2 the GOD I will always Love
I Need Courage 4 the Task
You told me all I had 2 do was Ask
Pretty Please remove the Fear
Let these Words Touch your Ear
So Lord tell me Good Things I need 2 Hear
Give me More Courage than I had last Year
4 the Bravest Heart is what I Pray
In the **House of Courage** is where I stay
Save me with the Strength that Courage Gives
Let my Courage Breath make sure it Lives
Because Retreating is something I just can't do
2 my Calling let me be True
Because everything I get I get from you
On the **Bubble Gums of Courage** is what I wish 2 Chew
I Promise 2 be Afraid No More
As the **Spirit of Courage** begins 2 Pour
GOD you Taught Me 2 be Courageous
Make Mother Courage Contagious
Hole me when I begin 2 Stumble & Fall
It's Crunch Time so throw me the Ball
Give me the Courage that I need
Plant in me that Bravery Seed
Give me the Encouragement that I need
As I take the Lead
2 Come Against Hate & Greed
Courageous is Written on My T Shirt
I'm **Captain Courageous** is what I Shout & Blurt
Because on my *Spiritual Knees* with GOD is how I so often Flirt
Who Formed me in my Mother's Womb
So I'm not afraid of the grave because I'm Brave
Because my Life Has already been Saved!

Prayer 4 Direction

Lord I need 2 know which way I need 2 Go
Do I Go High or **Do I Go Low?**
I just don't won't 2 be <u>Misguided</u> anymore
Hurry because my *Spiritual Feet* are getting Sore
Like Daniel Boone I Love 2 Explore
Touch my Spirit
Your Voice let me Hear It
Lead Me 2 Heaven not that Fiery Pit
The Bulls Eye of your Heart is what I Wish 2 Hit
So *Direct Me* like the Wind
<u>My Directions is what I need you 2 send</u>
Let them Break out of their Cocoon & Shell
You can Scream or You can Yell
I just don't want 2 Go the Wrong Way
Be my Coach & <u>Call the Perfect Play</u>
Lord be the Captain of my Soul
Let my Directions Begin 2 Unfold
Am I on the Right Intersection?
Who do I Vote 4 in the Election?
Be the Usher & get me 2 the Right Section
The Preacher didn't Know so I'm coming 2 You
Because your Directions are <u>Always Tried & True</u>
Like Dorothy the **Yellow Brick Road** is what I need 2 See
No Toll Bridges only Roads that are Free
Guide Me 2 that **Spectacular Place of Rest**
I don't want **Red Marks** on my Test
Hold my hand & Lead me Safely through
<u>I Love You & I Know You Love Me 2</u>
My GOD is who you Be
So Lord will you Hear my Plea?
HEAR **Him**, **Her**, **Them** & **Me**
Show Me the fastest & Easiest way 2 Grow
Move Me like the River Flow
2 the Right Place on the Map
Lay my Instruction in my Lap
Thanks Lord 4 all your Help
4 Always Saying YES & YELP
Lead Me Right *Steer Me* Left
Thanks 4 the Breath & a **Better Knowledge of Myself**
My Directions is what I just pulled off the Shelf
As GOD *Directs Me* like one of Santa elves!

PRAYER 4 FAITH

On the **GOD of FAITH** is who I cry out 2
Because without you there's nothing I can Do
Give me O' Lord a **FAITH** that's Tried & True
Give me **FAITH** when Life is beating me **Black** & **Blue**
On the **Bones of FAITH** let me Chew
Because it's sure 2 pull me threw
<u>I BELIEVE in the unseen</u>
Even though I don't know what everything means
Let my **FAITH** conjure up those Invisible Things
Let it Soar on Eagles Wings
Give me the Things that having **FAITH** Brings
I Pray O'LORD 4 **Eyes & Heart of FAITH**
That's willing 2 do whatever it Takes
Yes I'm FREE from worry of Mistakes
As I Depend on the **Faithfulness of FAITH**
Because She Promises never 2 crumble or break
Give me FAITH Give me FAITH is what I SAY
Give me More than I had Yesterday
Give me Enough 4 today
Be my *SHIELD* that keeps the enemy at Bay
Let my **FAITH** be a Sweet Smelling AROMA
That keeps my doubts in a Life Long Coma
O' FAITH would you live in me?
Give me a **FAITH** that the Whole World can see
Because your **Faithful Warrior** is who I be
Let my **FAITH** continue 2 GROW
Take it High when it's getting Low
Bury my Unbelief 6ft Below
Under Dirt & Snow
Thanks LORD 4 Making *My FAITH GREAT*
As I Sit & Wait with the Right Bait
On the **Breakfast of Faith** is what I just ate
As I walk Confidently through HER Gates
Leaving behind & unbelief because it's what **FAITH** Hates!

PRAYER 4 FAMILY & FRIENDS

This is **My Prayer** 4 my **Family & Friends**
GOD on your Grace & Mercy is what we Depend
4 their <u>Safety & Protection</u> is what I Pray
Let **Your Angels** be by their side each & Every Day
Keep them from all those <u>Invisible Things</u> that try 2 harm
Cover them while they experience their Thunder Storm
Be there 2 Grab them by the ARM
Supply my **Family & Friends** Every Need
I'm Praying because **My Prayers** are a Seed
Let them Know what Kind of GOD you are
<u>Heal Every Sickness</u> ***Heal Every Scar***
Reserve a Place 4 them in Heaven Above
Show my **Family & Friends** much Love
Hear **My Prayers** & Lord ***Please don't delay***
I'll Rejoice when you Make a Way
Give Ear O' LORD 2 my Beckoning Call
Be there when we Stumble & Fall
As I Include in **My Prayers** All & All
Because with you there's nothing 2 Big nothing 2 Small
Give my **Family & Friends** something *Good 2 Eat*
Beautiful Shoes 4 their Feet
Light Gas Water & Heat
Clothes that are Nice & Neat
And a Place 2 Comfortably lay their Head
With the Softest Bed
LORD I Know you heard what I said
<u>Let us ALL be Spirit Led</u>
<u>Let US ALL BE ONE</u>
Let us have FUN because ***WE WON***
And Believe in your SON
Thanks LORD 4 my **Family & Friends**
When it comes 2 **Family & Friends**
I Give Mine a <u>Perfect 10!</u>

PRAYER 4 FORGIVENESS

O' Gracious Father who dwells in the Heart
At the <u>Mercies of Forgiveness</u> is where I Start
Because that's the only thing that can keep us apart
Forgive me 4 all those things not done Right
Because all my sins are Locked in your sight
So <u>Forgive Me</u> as I ask with all my Might
Let my Prayers Reach the Highest Height
Let *THIS PRAYER* Reach the Bounty of your EAR
Let YOUR Grace & Mercy always be Near
Give my Empty Heart a Reason 2 Cheer
<u>Free Me</u> from any Discord or Dislike
So I'm telling unforgiveness 2 take a Hike
Let each one Forgive the other
From Brother Sister 2 Father & Mother
Don't allow me 2 Keep a Grudge
Because you are the Only Judge
Who Forgives us 4 all our sins
You now consider us Friends
You're unforgiving is the reason you're miserably Living
Because Negative Energy is what your Giving
So I Forgive all those who have done me wrong
Let Forgiveness be the only Song
The <u>Message of Forgiveness</u> is not 2 be Aborted
Forgive All is the NEWS Brief that was Reported
When we Forgive OTHERS we also Extend it 2 OUR SELF
As I put unforgiveness on the Eternal Shelf
Because it has no Breath Left
I Pray 2 Forgive the Unforgiving
Because Love & <u>Forgiveness Keeps Us Living</u>
Forgiveness is what I will always be Giving
O' LORD search the Depths of my Soul
<u>Release Me</u> from unforgiveness so I can be made whole
The Flags of Forgiveness has been raised up the Pole
Because unforgiveness is buried in that 6ft Hole
<u>2 be Forgiven we must Forgive</u>
Being a Forgiver is the only way 2 LIVE!

PRAYER 4 GOOD HEALTH

LORD <u>Keep me Healthy</u> & <u>Keep me Fit</u>
Be with me Everywhere I Walk & Sit
Keep Every disease & Every sickness out my way
Let me Healthier than I was Yesterday
Teach Me how 2 Better *Take Care of Myself*
I Wish 2 be in the *Best of Health*
I Desire 2 be just like Thee
I have the Holy Spirit so that makes Us a We
Cover Me in your Precious Blood
Wash Me with Your Spiritual Suds
Help Me eat the Right Things
Give Me the Joy that Healthiness Brings
Give Me Extra Air in my Heart & Chest
Let me always *Pass the Health Test*
Let me be the Captain of Zeal & Zest
So Lord I Thank You in Advance
4 being able 2 **sing rap jump run** & **dance**
With More Stamina than that Biker Lance
Let Me <u>Love 2 Exercise</u>
So sickness can't take me by Surprise
Keep Me at the Perfect Size
Let Me Be *Good 2 the Eyes*
So <u>Good Health</u> Come 2 Me
Because I want 2 Be as Healthy as can Be
All Body Functions are in Proper Order
Which gives me *Energy 2 Play*
<u>I'm HEALTHY</u> so Every day is a Holiday
O' LORD Give Me Healthy Habits 2 Live By
I Want 2 *Live a Long Time* is the Reason Why
They say it's even Healthy 2 Sometimes CRY
GOD Thanks 4 Getting Me in Shape
As I eat vegetables fruits & grapes
Because in <u>Perfect Healthiness</u> is where I Dwell
<u>If you're not Exercising GOD is who I'm Going 2 Tell!</u>

PRAYER 4 THE GOVERNMENT

O' GOD Please **Help Us** in our *Time of Need*
Plant in the Government <u>One Good Seed</u>
With a ***Good Heart Indeed***
Use the Government 2 ***Help the People*** 2 Succeed
Let not a another Solider have 2 Die or Bleed
Give Us ***A President*** who Knows how 2 Lead
<u>I Pray 4 All Our Elected Officials</u>
Let them not be quick 2 **Drop Bombs** & **Launch Missiles**
Let them <u>Create Jobs</u> that will Sustain the World
That will Help Every Boy & Every Girl
GOD I Pray 4 ***A Better Government***
One that is Heaven Sent
One that will let Us know where the Money Went
That will Share ***Every Dollar*** & ***Every Cent***
4 our sins <u>Let Us REPENT</u>
Lead Us O' LORD 2 the Promised Land
Justice in the Government is what I Demand
Touch the Heart of the ***Chief Commander in Command***
So that He or She Cares & Understands
Let ALL Officials be on <u>One Accord</u>
And Give Us things we can Comfortably Afford
Show Us O' LORD a Better Way
4 our Government is what I Pray
That the People can Rely on & Trust
Let All evil doers return 2 the dust
Because ***Total Liberation*** is the Biggest Must
So I Pray 4 Governmental Burst
That will <u>Satisfy the Peoples Thirst</u>
Help Us make Laws that are ***Fair & Right***
Let our Government Finally See the Light
That makes our **Future Brighter than Bright!**

PRAYER 4 THE HOLY GHOST

2 THE Great Spirit who *Lives in us All*
Hear Me O' LORD when I Call
Throw me the SPIRIT like the Quarterback tosses the Receiver the Ball
In my Body is where I want the Spirit 2 Fall
Breathe on me so I can be Free
4 the **Holy Ghost** is my only Plea
Come on Lord Live on the Inside of Me
Then a <u>Super Human</u> is what I will be
Give me the Power that the **Holy Ghost** Brings
4 more of you is what I Shout & Sing
Like Jesus Baptize me with Fire
Pump up my Flat Tire
4 your Presence is what I Desire
Give it 2 me because you Care
Because without you who can bare
Into the Eyes of the **Holy Ghost** I want 2 Stare
So we can become the <u>Perfect Pair</u>
So let the **Holy Ghost** quickly Come
Because Heaven is where the Ghost comes from
<u>I Believe so I Receive</u>
Now every Goal I can Accomplish & Achieve
GOD Breathe your Breath on me
Then I will be able 2 Properly See
The **Holy Ghost** is what I Need
4 you my Heart now Bleeds
I Receive the **Holy Ghost** by Faith
LORD my Belief is my Only Bait
4 the **Holy Ghost** I can Hardly wait
As I Meet my Fate
As GOD serves up the Spirit on my Plate
Thanks GOD 4 this <u>Most Precious Gift</u>
On its Goodness I will continue 2 Drink & Sift
Because you just gave my Spirit & Body a **Much Needed Uplift!**

PRAYER 4 A MATE

Dear LORD of the Heavens Above
Send me Some1 who <u>Knows how 2 Love</u>
Let Her/Him Swoop down like a Lonesome Dove
Some1 who is willing 2 Give some ***Unconditional Love***
I Pray 4 the Perfect Mate 4 Me
Come on Lord let me see
The one you have Ordained 4 me
Because my Queen/King is who She/He BE
Get me Ready 4 the **Love of my Life**
The one that will be my Husband or Wife
Let Her/Him be kind and Extra Nice
Let Her/Him offer Good & Excellent Advice
The one that will always have my back
Who will take up the Slack
And not talk 2 much Smack
The ***Soul Mate*** who has *Spirit & Soul*
That will make my Life Complete & Whole
Who will Help me reach my ***Dreams & Goals***
Give me a Mate that will be Good 2 Me
Who can set my Mind & Body Free
Show me my number #1 Lover
Who Loves 2 play games under the cover
Let us be the same branch on the same Tree
Give Her/Him 2 me if you hear my Plea
So LORD will you ***Prepare Me 4 my Helpmate***
Who will have my Heart pumping at the Highest Rate
Let us have the Most Perfect Date
Let me **Fish 4 my LOVE** with the Right Bait
Come 2 me O' Great Helpmate of Mine
Because Together we **Brightly Shine**
I Found you in a Game of Hide & Seek
Let Her/Him be **Humble & Meek**
That will Help me be Strong when I'm feeling Weak
Thanks Lord 4 my Helpmate
And 4 never Showing up Late
And 4 Giving me the <u>Patience 2 Patiently Wait!</u>

PRAYER 4 OPPORTUNITY

2 my LORD is where I Direct this Prayer
Asking you 2 place me in **Opportunities Chair**
I come 2 you because *I Know You Care*
In the ***Face of Opportunity*** let me Stare
Lead me 2 the Place where I need 2 Be
More Opportunity is what I need 2 See
Because ***The Opportunistic is Who I Be***
As I Look 4 **Total Opportunity**
Give Me One Chance *2 Strut my Stuff*
One Opportunity is Enough
Let my Lyrics & Rhymes be Smooth & Not Rough
Release me from these Economical Handcuffs
Let me Always Perform at my Best
With much Energy & Zest
In me LORD would You Invest?
Let me *Pass the Opportunity Test*
Opportunity comes 2 the Opportune
Make it Soon as I Get in Tune
4 OPPORTUNITY IS ALL I ASK
Let Her Take OFF Her Mask
In Her Glory let me Bask
I See Many Opportunities Coming my Way
4 your Assistance is what I Pray
Thanks LORD 4 the Opportunities that you Give
Which Gives Me a Reason 2 Live
Once again all I ask 4 is ***ONE CHANCE***
Now it's up 2 me 2 Go Forward & Advance
I Got Opportunity is the Reason that **I DANCE**
Because **Opportunity** Gives Us ALL a Fighting Chance!

PRAYER 4 PURPOSE

2 the GOD of Heaven who Knows All & Sees All
4 my Purpose is the Reason that I Call
It's Me Roaming down the Hall
Is my Purpose short small large or tall?
Do I have 2 Scale another Wall?
Or Fall off my Horse like the Apostle Paul
I Pray 2 Know what 2 Be
Let the Vision become Clear 2 See
In my Dreams you can give me a Peek See
Because my Purpose Opens up my Life like a Master Key
I Pray 4 a Purpose that will bring you all the Glory
After All this is the Purpose 4 this Purpose Filled Story
My Purpose is 2 Get the Attention All on YOU
The GOD who is Tried & True
So the Finger Pointer is Pointing the Finger 2 YOU
Which is Something Brand New
Help Everyone Find out Why they are Here
Whisper our Purpose in our Ear
It's what our Heart wants 2 Know
Was I made 4 the Heat or 4 the Snow
Which Way Do I Go What Do I Do?
Will my days be Many or Will my days be Few
Just let me Accomplish what I'm Here 2 Do
Yum Yum I See the Birth of my Purpose Coming
It's the Reason I Started Humming
My Purposed has been Summoned
And it's so Uncommon
I have work that needs 2 be done
And it's Going 2 be Fun in the Sun
Get your Purpose because my Purpose Got Me
True 2 Myself is what I got 2 be
2 Yourself My Friend Always Be True
No Matter what you Do or Don't Do
Remember the Heart holds the Clue
Your Purpose is what You LOVE 2 Do the Most
Just Get the Help & Aid of the Holy Ghost
I Found My Purpose so I BOAST
SO 2 GOD I MAKE MY TOAST!
THANKS A LOT!

PRAYER 4 A SOUND MIND

2 the Most High GOD I make my Request
In *My Mind* I invite you 2 be my Guest
As I Journey through this Life Long Quest
I Pray 4 a Mind that <u>Performs at its Best</u>
That Aces Every Trial & Every Test
A Mind Filled with *Utopia & Perfect Rest*
With a Body filled with *Energy & Zest*
Give *My Mind* the Needs it Desires
I'm *The Problem Solver* so I put out all Fires
Rotate *My Mind* like a Good Set of Tires
Let me Motivate & Inspire
B4 my time on this Earth Expires
4 a <u>Sound Mind</u> is what I Pray
Hear O' Lord what I Say
Make Famous the saying GREAT DAY! GREAT DAY!
Let that Lord Jesus kind of Mind be in Me
Give me *Spiritual Eyes* 2 Properly See
Because *My Mind* is the Key 2 me being Free
So let me be the Person I'm suppose 2 Be
I want a Mind that can figure any Problem out
That's Free of Worry & most of all Free of Doubt
That Soars like the Wild Eagle
Let *My Mind* Love 2 Mix & Mingle
If I were a Musical Note I'd be the Perfect Jingle
My Mind was built 4 Perfect Peace
So all Negativity must come 2 a cease
<u>The Mind of GOD</u> is what I Posses
In my LIFE GOD would you Invest?
Let me always *Satisfy & Impress*
And let me begin 2 worry less & less
My Mind is what I want you 2 Bless
Give me O'LORD a Mind Like Yours
B4 I'm done let me FINISH ALL my Earthly Chores!

PRAYER 4 THE ENVIRONMENT

2 the GOD of Everything that Breathes
2 the GOD who made the **Sun Moon Trees** & it's Leaves
I Pray 4 a Cleaner World
With the Help of Every Boy & Every Girl
I'm asking 4 a **World Wide Make Over**
Throw me my Tools & I'll Fetch like Rover
<u>Clean up the Earth is</u> what I'm trying 2 SAY
Because we didn't Find the Earth this Way
Pollution making the Day seem like the Night
My Neighborhood what a Horrible sight
Trash & Paper on the Ground isn't Right
Even the Birds done took Flight
Protect the swamps where the mosquito's Love 2 Bite
Give us O' LORD <u>Fresh Air</u> 2 take In
With the Environment I want 2 be Friends
Let the Angels of Beauty <u>Beautify the Land</u>
Get us back 2 the **Promised Land**
Let the Environment be Transformed into a Picture of Grace
O' Mother Nature put things back in their Proper Place
My Prayers are here 2 Fight the Environments Case
Because the *Foundation of the Earth* is our <u>Home Base</u>
So it's Time 2 Treat Her as if She is our ACE
<u>I Pray that ALL will join in on the Movement</u>
2 Better our Environment
So I Pray 4 our Government
That they will get the Poetic Message that was Sent
So Get In Tune with the Cosmos
And with the Wind that Blows
Down the Drain is where our mess Goes & Flows
Clean the Environment until She Glows
4 our Negligence I Repent
Because we're not the Owners we just Rent
One Lifetime that I know of is all there is 2 be Spent
So Spend it Well is Story that I Tell
Take care of the Environment is what I Yell
Are you Blind & Need 2 Read Brail
That you can't see we turned the Earth into HELL!

PRAYER 4 THE SICK

2 THE Great Healing **GOD of the Sky**
Healing is what I need from the Spiritual Pie
In Sickness I will not Believe the lie
Because my **GOD is a Healer** is Why
Who took Sickness away Captive
Hey my Faith is Alive & Active
Jesus Died that we may Live
Look at the Power LOVE gives
I Pray 4 all those who are on their sick bed
Let your *Healing Angels* touch their Head
Bye - Bye sickness you're as Good as Dead
In JESUS NAME & I Hope you heard what I Said
By the Spirit of GOD is how we are Led
LORD Help the sick
Give sickness & disease the Hardest Kick
And let us Not be Afraid
GOD says raise up from where you are Laid
Because the Price has already been Paid
Like GOD is how we are Perfectly Made
I Pray 4 the sick 2 be Healed
Let the Pain & Grief be Stilled
Because sickness FATE has been Sealed
Sickness has been Murdered & Killed
On its way 2 the pits of hell
BE HEALED! BE HEALED! Is what I Yell
Lord Heal like the **Great Healer** that you are
Sickness you're stalled like an out of Gas car
A Fallen Star covered in mud & tar
I Rejoice 4 the Healing that I Received
You were Healed because You & I Believed
By Faith I Believed this Prayer has been Received
GOD has Blessed us with the **Miraculous Power 2 Heal**
No Faking it's All So REAL!

PRAYER 4 TRUTH

4 the **TRUTH** is what my Heart longs 4
Because I don't want 2 Live lies anymore
On the **Highest Levels** of **TRUTH** is where I Wish 2 Be
Place the **TRUTH** in my Face so I can Clearly see
Let my Heart be Discerning 2 what is Right
I know **TRUTH** is a Beautiful Sight
It's the **Perfect Light**
On the Flesh of **TRUTH** is what I Desire 2 Bite
As **TRUTH** sends falsehood 2 Flight
I want **TRUTH** like ring around the collar
I yearn 4 it more than that *Mighty Dollar*
I Pray 4 what I need 2 Know
TRUTH is what I want 2 Follow
Wind of **TRUTH** let me feel your Blow
Because I Love your *Distinguished Glow*
And the way you Cut High & the way you Slice Low
Let those *Truthful Bells Ring*
Because I like the way She Sings
Give me **TRUTH** because it makes Life Better
I Pray 4 All True's 2 Come Together
4 the **TRUTH** is what I Yell
Tell me Lord where has **TRUTH** fell
I'm digging 4 **TRUTH** like Bushes Oil Wells
Lies are like a Train that's Derailed
From the School of Life lies have been Expelled
Thanks Lord because **TRUTH** & I have Finally Gelled!

PRAYER 4 UNCONDITIONAL LOVE

The GOD of Agape Love is whom I come 2
I Pray 4 LOVE because LOVE comes from you
Let me do what LOVE is suppose 2 Do
Which makes the Spirit & Body Feel Brand NEW
I Pray 2 be Loved with <u>Unconditional Love</u>
A LOVE that made its way from Heaven Above
That's the Type of LOVE I'm Looking 4
As I Continue 2 Ask 4 More & More
I Pray that Your LOVE will be Allowed 2 have FREE Course
4 <u>Unconditional Love</u> *is why I Raise my Voice*
Let LOVE be Mankind's 1ˢᵗ & Last Choice
From hate let the World divorce
And let US Return 2 Loves Main Power Source
I Pray 4 a LOVE that I can Feel
That's Realer than Real
2 its Power I Bend & Kneel
Because it's the *Perfect Pain Pill*
GODS Guaranteed Seal
The Ace of Love is the Card I've been Dealt
<u>GOD Touched me</u> *so I know how it Felt*
It's the *BEST FEELING EVER*
It made me Smart it made me Clever
I Pray 2 Love myself that I might be able 2 <u>LOVE OTHERS</u>
Let LOVE reach Every Sister & Every Brother
Onto the Laws of Love is what I hang on 2
Because LOVE is the Truest True
Thanks LORD 4 the LOVE that you so often Give
Which Helps me Better Live
Because <u>Unconditional Love</u> *is the Most Positive!*

PRAYER 4 WORK

LORD GOD of the Heavens & the Earth
Who gave Adam Work 2 Do 1st
4 Employment is what I Thirst
I Pray 4 the **Right Situation** 4 Me
Give me something 2 do like shade coming from the Tree
Lord Guide & Order my Steps 2 the Right Door
Because without Employment I will have 2 remain poor
Give me a Job that is able 2 pay all my Bills
And make sure I have enough Left over 2 Entertain & Thrill
So *I Pray 4 Higher Wages* in the work force
Without jobs poverty will continue 2 take its course
Give us **Nice Occupations** as I Lift up my Voice
Let us O' LORD *Breathe Sounds of Relief*
Because in your Justice is our Main Belief
LORD you Know Exactly what I need
So let my Prayers Grow like Well Nurtured Seeds
GOD with you by my side
I will have so Many Job Offers it will be Hard 2 Decide
Because on FAITH & LOVE is how I Ride
When I get my Work let me **Work it the BEST**
2 My Prayers please Say YES
Because I Heard You Love 2 Bless
I Believe in You GOD I Must Confess!

PRAYER WHEN YOU LOST SOME1 TO DEATH

Father I offer up the Sacrifice of Praise
From Death is how Jesus was Raised
By the Thoughts of Death he was unfazed
Because on the Promised Land he had Already Gazed
When Death comes Let Me Not Lose My Mind
Understanding is what I'm trying 2 Find
Help Me O' Lord with this loss
Clean me out like Dental Floss
Comfort Me in my Time of need
Seal up the leaking Heart that Bleeds
Because my Loved One has been *Spiritually Freed*
Let not Death cause me so much Grief
Who Knows Death could be a Better Kind of Relief
They are in Heaven is My Tattooed Belief
I Pray 4 Strength when the Time Comes
I Need Comfort is where I'm coming from
I now see Death as a Good Thing
When those **Heavenly Bells** begin 2 Ring
Because you've been 2 EARTH & Now you're Back
Heaven is your Trophy & Plague
So be not Afraid of this thing we call Death
When it comes 2 Victory it's the Last Hurdle Left
So I Praise GOD while I still have breath Left
I know you lost someone close 2 you
It's OK 2 Boo Hoo
But let not Death Get the Best of you
Because dying is what we all one day must do
Death is when the body goes into its Eternal Sleep
But the Spirit it can't Keep
So don't let Death play you cheap
Because Death is something we all have 2 Reap
Live because Life is 4 the Living
Positive Things about Death is what I'm Giving
Because one thing Death can't Do is **STOP the Living from Living!**

PRAYER 4 INCOME

Lord I'm coming 2 you 4 a **Financial Blessing**
And I have no time 4 2nd Guessing
Shoot poverty with your Spiritual Smith & Wesson
Because it's already taught me a valuable Lesson
Lord the Bills are Due & **I Need your Help**
You Promised 2 Handle the Next Step
In Heaven is where all the *Wonderful Blessings* are Kept
So I now Pray 4 More Income
Because you're **The Source** from which all Blessing come from
You can Give me all or you can Give Me Some
Fatten up my Pockets like Fat Albert's Big Thumb
Forgive Me Lord if I need 2 Repent
But all my Money is Gone & Spent
Give Me What I Need
As I water this Prayer Seed
You can do it Slow or you can do it Fast
Just let my Future be Better than my Past
Give me a supply that will always Last
Blow up Poverty with the Biggest Blast
4 more Income is what I Pray
That will get me Comfortably through the day
And keep the Bill Collectors at Bay
Lord **I Trust In You O YES I DO**
Thanks 4 coming through
Which is what you always do
Because can't no one Bless, Bless like You!

PRAYER AGAINST DEPRESSION

I come 2 you O' GOD with the Heaviest Heart
Asking you 2 Remove that Depressing Dart
Because the Hurt is tearing my Life Apart
I'm Depressed & I'm not making Decisions that are Smart
So I Need you 2 Clean My Heart
I Pray 2 be Released from this <u>Nasty Disease</u>
I'm on my Knees begging you Please
Put my Depression on Freeze
2 my situation I know you have the Keys
Let me not try 2 sleep my Life away
For the Solution is what I Pray
That will push my unhappiness out the way
So I can Cheerfully Play
Lord help me figure out the cause
Because I'm stuck on Pause
Hurry because Depression brings about the Early Death
<u>Discontinue the Pain</u> take it off the Shelf
Because the Depression is causing me bad Health
Freedom is what I yearn
As I do I Gigantic U Turn
In hell let my Depression Burn
Please LORD handle my *Top Concern*
The opposite of Depression is Happy
Because being Depressed makes us Feel Crappy
Being Happy makes me <u>Feel Good</u>
Chop down my sadness like Chopped Dead Wood
Thanks LORD 4 Releasing me from my Great Depression
I'm Delivered is my True Confession
It's in Recession a cut out Page & Section
The Loser in the Election
Not even coming in my Direction
Thanks GOD because that's the <u>End of my Depression!</u>

PRAYER AGAINST DOUBT

O' Heavenly Father who reigns from On High
I'm beginning 2 Doubt & I don't know why
I've doubted so much I've began 2 Cry
So I'm going 2 give this <u>Praying Thing</u> a Try
Take away the Doubt that's crept into my Heart
Let it no longer tare my Life apart
I come 2 you GOD because you're so Smart
I Got Faith so let the Healing Start
You said if I Believed I would Receive
Because with Doubt nothing Gets Achieved
Don't let Doubt stop my Flow
I Pray 4 it 2 Go
LORD run my Doubt out of Town
Because I know it's causing you 2 frown
Set me Free if it has me Bound
Give me Belief because Belief Scores Touchdowns
I Pray 4 the Strength 2 Conquer the Unknown
Crack my Doubt like a split ice cream cone
Put up a sign that says <u>NO FLY ZONE</u>
Because Doubting will not be Condoned
Lord Give Me the Courage 2 BELIEVE
And let Us not be Deceived by those who Love 2 Deceive
Thanks Lord 4 <u>Taking Away my Doubt</u>
Like the Detergent Shout I had 2 Shout it Out
Because Doubt doesn't belong Here
So I no longer Fear
Thanks GOD 4 whispering <u>Don't Doubt in my Ear</u>
It's just what I needed 2 Hear
Thanks once again my Heavenly Friend
Because My Love 4 you will never End!

PRAYER FROM FEAR

2 the Spirit that is within Me
From Fear I wish 2 be Free
GOD I know All Courage comes from you
So **Out the Window** is where my Fear Flew
I Pray 4 the Strength 2 Face all my Fears
Help me avoid all Arrows & Spears
As I Destroy Fear B4 It comes Near
I'm cutting up Fear with my Spiritual Shears
Because GOD hasn't Given me the <u>SPIRIT OF FEAR</u>
I Refuse 2 be Afraid
Which gives me a passing Grade
<u>GOD & His Angels</u> Promise 2 come 2 my Aide
As the Fearful Thoughts Begin 2 Fade
LORD keep me from the Fears that hold me Back
Thanks Lord 4 being there 2 take up the Slack
With you by my side in no Area will I lack
That's why I **Speak Spoken Words** that ***Live & Attack***
Let not Fear Rob me of my Power
Let my Courage reach the Highest Tower
All my Fears is what I'm here 2 Face
As the Pitcher picks off Fear at 1st Base
That's as far as my fear is going 2 Get
Because GOD is pitching an He's yet 2 give up a Hit
The Uniforms of Courage is the Perfect Fit
<u>I'm Going 2 Heaven</u> so I'm not Fearing that Burning Pit
Take away my Fear because it doesn't know how 2 Steer
When Fear Leaves the Crowd begins 2 Cheer
I Thank GOD because ***My Fears are a Thing of the Past***
Because I done Feared my Last
Now I can have a Blast
Because GOD Got Rid of my Trash!

PRAYER 4 TOTAL UNITY

This is My Prayer 4 World Wide Unity
In Every Town & Every Community
LORD Let Us Begin 2 Hold Mighty Hands
All across the Land from Africa 2 Disney Land
No matter the Culture or Name brand
I Pray 4 Unity in our Churches Governments Schools & Homes
Because Unity makes the hair easy 2 Comb
It's more Sheltering than the Superdome
Total Unity is what I'm Calling 4
That will cause the People 2 Soar
So LORD Help us Complete this Hefty Chore
Come on GOD let Everyone Hear Your Roar
Show us how it's suppose 2 be Done
Like Jesus the Only Begotten Son
I Love the Peace that Only Unity can Bring
So let us *Come Together* when those Liberty Bells Begin 2 Ring
Unity of Spirit is what the Mass Choir began 2 Sing
I Pray that ALL PEOPLE will UNITE
It's Good because it's Right
Division you're about 2 Lose this Fight
Unity is the Democratic Day & *Division is the Notorious Night*
I Pray that ALL will give UNITY a TRY
So division I'm saying BYE- BYE
Unity is the Truth & division is the lie
Unity makes us Laugh division causes us 2 Cry
So UNITE All GOD'S PEOPLE of the Earth
If you want 2 come in 1st
And Quench our Thirst
It's a Party because UNITY is about 2 Burst!

PRAYER 4 PEACE ON EARTH

2 the GOD of Peace I make my Petition
Because with you is the Final Decision
Let <u>Peace on Earth</u> *be the Soldiers Mission*
Hostility & War it's time 2 take a Shower
As Peace Blossoms into the Perfect Flower
Lord Give Me Relaxation in my Spirit
My Prayer is that you Hear it
Listen 2 the Tone of my Voice
<u>Peace & Love</u> **is my 1st Choice**
4 the Rewards of Peace is what I seek
Over the Waterfalls of Life She takes Her Peek
Peace it's me Calling out your Name
Let *Peace of Mind* **be the Game**
Send disruption & division back 2 hell
<u>Be Peaceful</u> *is what my Spirit YELLS*
Give Me Peace at work home & in the streets
Let the <u>Gospel of Peace</u> **be at my Feet**
Let us Dance 2 the Right Beat
Come on Peace Clean us Up Nice & Neat
Help Us Lord 2 Obtain our Goal
Give Us our Peace which the devil Stole
Let War come 2 a Halt & Cease
With no need of the Police
Let there be Perfect Peace
Between the Animal & Beast
From the Greatest 2 the Least
Peace on Earth is my Final Plea
Come on LORD Set the World Free
Peace is Heaven & Heaven is Peace can't you See?
It surely Sounds Good 2 Me
Because the <u>Peace Maker</u> *is Who I BE!*

PRAYER 2 KNOW GOD

2 the GOD of the Unknown
I'm Dialing you up on my <u>Spiritual Telephone</u>
My Hope is that you will <u>Make Yourself Known</u>
YOU are who I wish 2 Know
Because that would put me in that ***Perfect Flow***
GOD you are the <u>Star of the Show</u>
Say YES & Please don't say NO
On your Vine is where I Desire 2 Grow
Come on Lord make it All Clear
Whisper Gently in my Ear
Your Words is what I need 2 Hear
I Need You is All I'm trying 2 Say
2 the GOD of the Night & **the GOD of the Day**
Let ***Wonderful Knowledge*** of You come my Way
And Please let there be no Delay
Reveal Yourself 2 what you have Made
Let the **MYSTERY** begin 2 Fade
<u>In Knowing You</u> give me a ***Passing Grade***
I just want 2 Know who you <u>Truly Are</u>
Are you Near or **Are You Far?**
Where do you stay Where do you Be?
Visions of You is what I Wish 2 See
<u>Let Everyone Know You Not Just Me</u>
Because you're the Only One who can Set Us Free
I Pray 2 See You in Your Glory
Then I can Release my Worry
I Pray 2 Know the <u>Author of this Story</u>
The GOD of Heaven **the GOD of Earth** is whom I Need
On Your Goodness let me Feed
I Seek You with All My Heart
Because you are ***The BEGINNING*** & ***The START***
So let the *Curtains of Mystery* be pulled Apart
<u>A Deep Relationship</u> is what I'm Looking 4
I want 2 Know You down 2 your Very Core
So Knowing You will be my Only Chore
GOD I Just Want 2 Know That I Know That I Know I Know You
Because when it comes <u>2 Creators</u> you're **The TRUE!**

THE WICKED LIGHT IS PUT OUT!

It's time 4 the wicked 2 hit the road

Yes I'm kicking you out in the cold

Move you're not wanted here anymore

You're vacant like a closed down store

A lion that's lost its roar

A pimpless whore whose pantyhose are tore

You've been out done you stinky son of a gun

Your light is about 2 lose it shine

So go 2 the bench head 4 the pine

Because you've been caught in your own bind

The wicked light is put out can't you see

He no longer holds the key

Wake up and realize that you are free

His **Day of Judgment** is here

You devils have a right 2 fear

What was done in the dark has come 2 the light

As you vanish from the people's sight

You're not right so put your dukes up it's time 2 fight

The Victory has been won

Thanks 2 GOD'S only begotten Son

The wicked light is put out is what I shout

No longer able 2 sprout with no more clout

GLORY 2 GOD the wicked light is put out!

♥ Wisdom Come ♥

1.   You can't pray and worry at the same time. Either you're doing the one or either you're doing the other! Don't let worry break down your immune system! Worry has taken many to and early grave!

2.   Pray with the belief that GOD hears your prayers and don't stop praying until you feel better! Now that's what I call real prayer!

3.   Jesus said feed my lambs! Jesus said take care of my sheep! Jesus said feed my sheep! John 21:15 Spiritual food heals weary souls!

4.   Jesus made me do it! My action reflect the one of whom I look up 2!

5.   A man should never be ashamed to own up to that he has been in the wrong which in other words is saying I'm wiser than I was yesterday!

6.   Wisdom outweighs any wealth! As a matter of fact Wisdom is Wealth!

7.   Who you are when times are toughest gives you a good indication of who you truly are on the inside!

8.   Life is like weight lifting without resistance the muscles don't grow! Inactivity makes one weak!

9.   What we've done for ourselves alone dies with us but what we've done for others and the world remains and is immortal!

10. Life gives you what you give it! Help someone!

11. Faith will work without prayer but prayer will not work without a Living Faith!

12. Remember my friend GOD has the power to do anything! We only limit GOD by our limited beliefs!

13. PRAYER aint never hurt no one!

14. Nothing staying the same can change!

15. Continued difficulty says something isn't right and that change is needed! When people change the world will change!

16. He who has lost his hope has truly lost everything!

17. Knowing my situation is going to get better gives me a reason to keep fighting for my sanity in an insane world!

18. Taking risk is a risky business but if risk is not taken progress is halted and no forward movement is made! So I risk all to get all!

19. Don't let fear stop you from growing!

20. She who is broken hearted from past relationships is truly broken! To fix the hurt one must be truthful about how you feel because covered scars never heal! It will be ok!

21. Ask the question was I born to die or was I born to live because most live in fear of death some fear life but he that liveth in fright is dead already! Fear not!

22. Our Heavenly Teacher has the answer to the test your going through! Every problem comes with a Answer so with all your heart seek the Problem Solver!

23. GOD is only as real as you believe he is and GOD can only do what you think he can do!

24. Trust me my friend impossible is nothing to him who Thinks its possible!

25. Failure is not an option to him who is determined to Succeed! Be determined because determination determines the final out come of unfinished business!

26. A nation is only as good as its head! To get life right we must get our head right because a new head brings forth new things! So rejoice better days are ahead!

27. Whatever challenges we face together we most assuredly erase! The Unity of Teamwork is the cure for the socials ills of the world! Get ready to do your part!

28. Is it me or can you feel the Positive Energy of Hope in the air! Effective speakers leave crowds filled with hope in hopeless situations! Hope is Alive!

29. Don't be misled bad company corrupts good manners! 1Corithains 15:33. Who we hang around is a great indication of who we are and what we are about! Your friend is a mirror! Because we hang around those who most resemble us!

30. Cowardly abusers only beat those weaker than themselves because insecurity is their middle name! May GOD rescue that abused soul from a life of hell!

31. Who can say I have kept my heart pure. I am clean and without sin? Proverbs 20: 9 That goes to show you no one has the right to judge another person WE all fall short!

32. The ultimate measure of a man is not where he stands in moments of comfort and convenience but where he stands at times of challenge and controversy! Martin Luther King

33. Faith by itself if it is not accompanied by action is dead! Faith has us moving and doing things to bag up our belief because dead things don't move!

34. In the darkest moments of our lives is when GODS Light shines brightest!

35. Do not accept the worries of the mind and watch the illusions of fear fade away!

36. He who conceal his sins does not prosper but whoever confesses and renounces them finds mercy! Proverb 28:13

37. Being an open book of truth can put you in good standings with GOD!

38. If any one says I love GOD yet hates his brother he is a liar for anyone who does not love his brother whom he has seen can not love GOD whom he has not seen! John 9:18

39. The best medicine for depression is motivation because motivation jumpstarts hearts which in turns gives the broken in spirit a reason to live! I got the cure!

40. IMPROVEMENT compels us to improve! If we're not getting better then we're getting worse! To stay the same is and miserable existence! IMPROVE!

41. GOD told me to tell you he loves you unconditionally and that a place in heaven has been reserved just for you! GOD said everything's going to be ok!

42. May the GOD of Heaven do Heavenly things in your life! May the Powerful Spirit of Goodness move Powerfully in your life! Be Strong!

43. A Happy Heart makes the face cheerful but heartache crushes the spirit! Proverbs 15:13 Do what makes your Heart Happy so you can Truly Smile!

44. When we Include GOD we Exclude the devil! Get GOD involved and your problem are solved because nothing is too hard for GOD! Peace to you and yours!

45. Unexpressed feelings depress the Spirit which zaps the body of all its power!

46. Speak your pain to release your pain! That's called Praying!

47. In ordered to do a job the right way GODS going to let you do it the wrong way then when you know how it's not done then you will get closer 2 how its suppose 2 done!

48. He who tries to take on this crazy world alone on his own will surely moan and groan! We weren't built to be alone we were created for each other!

49. The only way to beat negative things is with positive things! Set your mind on positive things and watch the Positive Stuff that it brings! GROW!

50. What we see on the outside is just a shadow of what's on the inside of us! To Beautify the Outer we must first Beautify the Inner! Peace to you!

51. What frightens us if taken on will Enlighten us!

52. Fear faced is fear Erased! Be big enough to face your fears!

53. The best way to calm an uneasy spirit is to do something good for someone else!

54. The best way to be Encouraged is to Encourage someone else! BE STRONG!

55. He who trust everyone will have many heartbreaks but He who trust no one finds it HARD to enjoy life!

56. In relationships when Trust goes Love goes!

57. The Spirit of the LORD will come upon you in power and you will prophesy with them and you will be changed into a different person!1 Samuel 10:6 BE RENEWED!

58. If the Light of Hope is shining in our heart and mind even the darkness of this world will be Light to you!

59. Keep Hope alive if you wish to survive!

60. Self knowledge + Self Love + Self Motivation = High Self Esteem!

61. He who can master Self is Free from the bondage of the unmerciful!

62. He who is without family becomes easy prey for the enemy whose job it is to breakup families! Heal our families Lord!

63. Let us not become hard like concrete in our thinking but soft like clay which is able to be reshaped and reformed! May the Hand of GOD be on you!

64. Anger has hurt written all over it and the only thing hurt can do is hurt because to be hurt hurts! May we overcome those things that hurt!

65. Faith is having the unwavering ability to see the end result of what you desire to happen even though it looks like its not going to happen! Believe!

66. No one get anywhere without first knowing where he or she is going!

67. Either your going forward or your going backward our like a crazy man going in circles! Know what you Want and Go Get It!

68. I know that whatever problem or tough situation you may be experiencing I tell you this : Its not bigger than GOD! Nothings too hard for GOD!

69. He who is happy is happiest when making others happy! If you want to be happy you got to get around some one happy it will rub off on you I promise!

70. As a magnet attracts so does our Mind attract and bring to pass that which we think about most! So we should think on what we want not on what we don't want!

71. When I'm going through my tough times I keep telling myself I must Endure! I must Endure! I must Endure! Just like the little train that thought it could You Can!

72. I pray for GODS Goodness to make residence in your life and that the GOOD in your life will outweigh the bad! Be Well Balanced and yea expect Good News! Peace.

73. The closer you walk with GOD the farther we get from the devil!

74. Every struggle every pain every hurt every misunderstanding is to draw us nearer to GOD!

75. What GOD has for you is for you and can't nothing or no one take it from you!

76. Let it go if it comes back its yours if it doesn't it wasn't yours in the first place! GROW!

77. It takes two to argue one looks foolish fussing by himself! So always look for the opportunity to be the bigger person!

78. Peacemakers are Blessed with peace!

79. Are you looking at your problems from the viewpoint of an Giant or from the viewpoint of an ant? To the Giant all is small to the ant all is BIG! BE ENCOURAGED!

80. The most complete people are those who chose to turn their disadvantages into advantages!

81. Don't play the victim but play the role of the overcomer! GROW!

82. The Right Words at the Right Time said the Right Way is sure to make Things Alright!

83. May the Spirit of GOD send you what you need to be Uplifted and Spirit and Soul!

84. He who Believes in himself finds it easy to Believe in others!

85. If I can then you can if you can then I can because one Spirit formed and made us all! I Believe in you!

86. What goes in must come out! We cry to release, we pray to release, we scream to release, we exercise too release! We boo boo to release! Whatever you do (PLEASE RELEASE)!

87. Many good intentions are started but very few are finished! Don't allow the obstacles the (HARDKNOCK) to abort your mission! Stand the test of time Get up and Finish!

88. He who listen with his ears and hears with his heart will Heal his Spirit and Bless his Soul!

89. Listeners don't go through as much unnecessary pain as non-listeners do!

90. Hold your head up! Hang in there! Trouble don't last always! You can do it! Everything's gone work itself out!

91. Don't give up! GOD is in control! Be BLESSED!

92. Nothing in life cleanses the consciousness of a mans mind like being honest and telling the truth! If we allow it to the truth will set us free! GROW!

93. We go though life in stages which fade in and out at different points in our lives! You cant skip stages at some point you will have to go back and live that stage!

94. We must experience failure in life to appreciate Success in life! Don't let setbacks be the end but the beginning that propels you forward to bigger and better things!

95. Wish nothing on another that you would not want wished upon yourself!

96. People will do you wrong but don't blame them they just don't know no better! Give it to GOD!

97. You have the Power to overcome you have the Power to change you have the Power to heal you have the Power to be happy. You have the Power is all I'm saying! Use your Spiritual Powers!

98. If your not working a job that's your passion your not going to last very long!

99. I pray for better jobs with better bosses! Be patient God has something great in store for you!

100. It takes work to make relationships work! The question is are you willing to put forth the time an effort required to make it work!

101. You got to give some You got to take some! So GROW!

102. Without money one must accept what ever the people who are in control will allow them to have!

103. Politics is money and money is politics! Money moves a lot of things!

104. The GOD of comfort, comfort his comforters so that they may be able to comfort the uncomfortable! May the Lord Comfort all the unstable minds of the world!

105. If we hold on to all past pains and hurts we will have no strength to handle future pains and hurt! Hurt is apart of life but Thank Goodness we can recover!

106. There's nothing too broken that GOD can't fix! Give what's broken in your life to the Creator if he doesn't fix it then it isn't meant to be fixed! Let the Fixer Fix It!

107. Who on earth is in any position to judge or criticize another for his short comings when we all do wrong things and come with flaws! Praise and Thank GOD for Mercy!

108. My high school coach use to tell us, You got to see yourself winning the game before the game! He won 51 games in a row! You got to first see it in your mind!

109. The Spirit is willing but the flesh is weak is the Truest Truth the bible ever made! The body only releases and let's goes of what it's tired of!

110. Is there any reward for being good is there any compensation for doing the right thing is there any benefit for believing in GOD? I think so but try it for yourself!

111. Something refreshing something new may GOD give you a clue of what to do!

112. Have a Great Day and don't forget to Pray and may the Spirit help you find your way!

113. Feeding the Spirit Uplifting and Hope giving words is the best medicine 4 the down and depressed Mind!

114. If you want what's Good you got to digest what's good because the Spirit is what the Spirit eats!

115. Whatever we want 4 ourselves we must be willing to give to another! If you want Encouragement Encourage someone else! If you want Happiness make someone else Happy! If you want Peace be Peaceful!

116. Life requires that we Give It before4 we Get It!

117. When something we want is just out our reach it keeps us reaching! When we stop reaching then we stop growing and when we stop growing we start dying! When we find something worth reaching 4 then we find something worth living for!

118. Unforgiveness is a heavy burden 2 carry around for so many years! Should he or she be Forgiven if he or she has been unforgiving of others!

119. Forgiving is not forgetting it's just not allowing what someone did to you in the past 2 weigh you down in the future! I WILL BE A FORGIVER!

120. GOD said Weeping may endure 4 a night but Joy comes in the morning!

121. Things that happen 2 us in this life will cause us 2 cry but GOD Promises us that there is something better on the other side of our pain!

122. I'm singing in my Spirit Trouble don't last always- Trouble don't last always!

123. 2 many times in relationships we look for things in a person that are just not there!

124. No matter how hard you try you can't turn an apple in2 an orange!

125. The Greatest challenge of Life is to keep getting back up when Life knocks you down! My Determination will not let me stay down!

126. Put up a fight and the devil will run away!

127. For Dreams and Goals 2 manifest one must SEE IT in his Mind SPEAK IT with his Mouth and DO IT with his Body! Faith without works is dead!

128. He who does not release and express how he or she truly feels is sure 2 remain clogged up on the inside!

129. What goes unexpressed keeps one depressed! I'm just letting go how I feel and IT FEELS GREAT!

130. None of us come without flaws everybody makes mistakes no one is perfect!

131. Do you have 2 be a saint to say anything about GOD because if you do I will not be able to talk anymore? As long as I have GODS Approval what the enemy says doesn't even matter!

132. Accept what GOD says about you not what man says about you! This is how you know when GOD or the devil is speaking GOD builds you up and the devil tares you down!

133. Let the weak say I am strong is what the bible says! A lot of times we say things about ourselves that weaken our ability to handle tough situations!

134. 2 overcome something you 1st must believe that you can overcome it! There is Victory in Good Self Talk!

135. He who does not know where he is going is headed nowhere!

136. Sometimes Life requires us to blaze our own trail meaning you might have to get off the path everybody else is on and make your own way!

137. We don't know what we can do until we do it but he who is afraid 2 step out will surely stay in the same place he's in for the rest of his life!

138.   GOD didn't give me the Spirit of fear so that's why I'm not afraid 2 try!

139.   Without risk there is no advancement!

140.   When we seek 2 hurt others for the hurt that they caused us the hurt will never go away!

141.   Acting in hurt doesn't work! All hurt knows how 2 do is hurt because it's hurt! Don't let your hurt, hurt you!

142.   Knowing who I am, knowing what I am and knowing why I am is the key 2 living a Fulfilling Life!

143.   When you know yourself you are able 2 know others! Knowing who you are gives you a Powerful Force!

144.   He who does nothing gets nothing every time!

145.   If you're not moving then you're standing still and no one gets anywhere in life by standing still!

146.   My mind is on letting my actions do the talking!

147.   When we come together WE WIN! When we UNITE WE WIN!

148.   Nothing beats teamwork but more TEAMWORK! There's no other answer to our problems! It's the simplest move we could make! If you're tired of losing lets be a Family!

149.   Once a person has experienced real and genuine Love anything less than that is not recognized!

150.   The Love I Love with is the Love GOD Loved me with!

151. No one likes pain but without pain GAIN is not accomplished! He who uses his pain to the benefit of others is Enlightened and Empowered with Understanding!

152. When things don't happen the way we want or think they should happen BELIEVE that GOD has a better plan with a better way! Know GOD Knows best!

153. No matter how bad the situation looks THINK POSITIVE! No matter what you have 2 endure THINK POSITIVE! A Positive Mental Attitude will get you far!

154. A Strong Minded person Mentally prepares himself for future events! The Strong are not afraid 2 think on their own! Give not your power 2 another!

155. We must accept responsibility for our own lives not blaming someone else for where we are or are not in our lives! Have that NO EXCUSES type of aAtitude!

156. When the heat is on When the storm arises the real you will appear! In pressure situations let the best you come 4th because you are better than you use 2 be!

157. Who can you Trust? Who can you run 2? If you don't have Family! Without Family one must stand alone! May GODS Spirit Perfectly fix our Family Matters!

158. Nothing or no one cries and screams louder and harder than he who is trapped in a seamlessly hopeless situation! Don't throw in the towel GOD has a plan!

159. The Life actions of a man tells the life story of the man! Our actions reveal our real identity!

160. We must better the inner man 2 better the outer man! He who believes in himself finds it easy to believe in others!

161. When people don't believe in you or doubt your abilities it's only because they have allowed someone else to shatter their dreams and because they can't do it they just figure you can't do it!

162. Never given up on our dreams and Aspirations gives us a reason to keep wanting 2 wake up in the morning! We must find that Motivation that keeps us going even though everything around us is all out of wack!

163. Resistance is what builds strong muscles!

164. What have I learned since high school? How much have I grown? What's my Purpose in life? Am I in the right place am I on the right track? These are the questions one must ask ones self if one wishes 2 grow! I refuse 2 stay the same! I must Learn I must Grow!

165. We are all energy so the energy that you give is the energy you will receive!

166. Our energy increases when our Happiness Increases!

167. Why do anything that doesn't bring you happiness because life is about being happy! If you're not happy then you're sad!

168. Truly Happy people make those around them Happy so if you're unable to find Happiness within yourself find someone who is Happy and its energy will rub off on you!

169. Happy people make the world better so I pray for more Happy people in the world!

170. Whatever you are Great at and Love doing is what you were created 2 do!

171. When things are tiresome and toilsome Life is just telling us Hey you are off the path of your purpose!

172. He who is waiting 2 be perfect before doing anything in GODS name will surely be waiting a long time!

173. If we say and do nothing because of our imperfection the enemy of GOD wins!

174. We come here equipped with all the necessary tools needed 2 Succeed! It's just up 2 that individual 2 develop his or her Talents!

175. Education makes one a valuable commodity!

176. Running away from our problems instead of dealing with them only prolongs them!

177. Either you're going 2 fight or take flight! Put up a fight and the devil cowers down!

178. We may feel like blaming GOD for the unhappy things that happen 2 us but Life's trials are the means by which we are Developed and refined! A Greater Good will come from it!

179. I know we are tempted 2 give up on people or situations that have not changed for years but it only takes an instant for GOD 2 change what seemed unchangeable! GOD IS POWERFUL!

180. You will know the Truth and the Truth will set you free! Falsehood bounds and locks you down! TRUTH Liberates and Sets you FREE ! May we be able 2 handle the Truth when it comes our way!

181. The Exercise of GRATITUDE will strengthen your Soul and Spirit! Be Grateful for what you have and more things to be Thankful for will come your way! Be GRATEFUL because it could be worse!

182. What I want and desire for myself I want and desire for others also! I want Peace! I want Happiness! I want Good Health! I want GOD ! I HOPE what I want is what you want!

183. In Helping you GOD is really Helping Himself because GOD Resides on the inside of Every Living Thing! If you hurt GOD hurts! So feel Better so our GOD can feel Better!

184. When death takes someone we Love its like 2 people died because the one left behind ceases 2 live also! How are you going 2 be sad for too long When you BELIEVE they are gone 2 a place Far Better!

185. Doing what you want 2 do is LIFE! There is no Satisfaction and there is no happiness in doing what you do not want 2 do!

186. If you want 2 BE HAPPY do what you want not what they want!

187. May the Creator of Life bring Wonderful Blessings your way! May the Most Beautiful Pictures of Peace be

Formed in your Mind! May your Prayers Reach the Ear of our Maker!

188. In moments of anger we tend 2 say and do things that we will later regret because HURT has no brakes! Don't hold it against them it was just their hurt talking!

189. All one can expect in life is 2 be treated and loved like he has treated and loved others in this world!

190. He is a fool who gives hate and expects 2 receive Love!

191. Saying something and doing something are 2 different things! One talks it the other walks it! If we can't walk what we talk then we shouldn't talk! I'm finna walk it out!

192. 2 Look outside your self for the answer 2 your dilemma is a fruitless act!

193. What's on the Inside of us is a Direct Result of what's on the Inside of us! IT'S A INSIDE JOB!

194. When GOD wants 2 Create a thing He Speaks that thing in2 Existence! The Mouth is a Powerful Force but one cannot Utilize what he has unless he knows what he has 1st!

195. My Mom Taught me how 2 Love People for What & How they were! That was Unconditional Love in Action! You Don't Teach Love You Show Love! I Love Like My Mom!

196. The Beautiful thing about Serving GOD is that you might not have Everything you wish you had but what

you need always seems 2 make it's way 2 you! Just when you need it most!

197. He who carries around a Mirror in his hand is able 2 see himself giving him no time 2 Criticize others for their mistakes because he is 2 busy Correcting himself! Where's your Mirror?

198. There is always a Harvest for the seeds that we have sown in the past! Be Patient some seeds take longer 2 Bud & Sprout than others! Nurture your seed in the Mean Time!

199. Blessed is he who has ears 2 hear & eyes 2 see! When we hear something Good we Feel Good & When we see something Good we Feel Good! I GOT THE GOODS!

200. Different View Points & Different Perspectives arise from having Lived in Different Environments! Lets Respect each others Differences! LOVE ME LOVE AS I AM!

201. He who is locked up is sad while he who is free is Happy!

202. He who does not Fight for his Freedom will remain a Slave for the rest of his Life!

203. If GOD can't Motivate you if GOD can't Heal you then my Faith is in vain & Life is not worth Living but if GOD can GOD Will!

204. A lot of people have asked me where I get all these beautiful words of wisdom from everyday! It comes from

My Pain! My Struggles! My experiences! My Heart! But Most of All It Comes from my Alone time with GOD!

205. If GOD is going 2 do anything in this world he is going 2 need a body 2 do it through! I Go where GOD Tells me 2 Go! My Life is not my Life anymore! GOD DONE TOOK OVER MY BODY!

206. He who is able 2 Balance his life will not live an Unbalanced Life! 2 much of something or 2 less of something can be dangerous but 2 get just the right portion is a Blessing! Find Balance & you find Happiness!

207. When life knocks you on your back GET BACK UP! When someone hurts your heart & bruises your mind GET BACK UP! When you find yourself at your lowest point GET BACK UP! We only lose when we don't GET BACK UP! GET BACK UP!

208. Running from our problems doesn't solve our problems it only prolongs them! Problems faced are problems erased! Watch out devil cause here I come!

209. He who has nothing good 2 say does good not 2 say nothing! Once words are spoken they cannot be taken back! SO HE WHO HOLDS HIS TONGUE IS WISE!

210. Good behavior does not have 2 be advertised because Goodness advertisement can be heard by the deaf, understood by dumb and seen by the blind!

211. Whatever you're good to will be good to you!

212. Forgiveness gives us excess to the throne room of GOD which is a Kingdom of MERCY!

213. A cheerful look brings JOY 2 the Heart & Good News Gives Health 2 the Bones! Proverbs 15:30 That goes 2 show us the Power of what Good Words can do 4 the soul!

214. Be Encouraged! Be Empowered! Be Uplifted! Be Enlightened! Be Motivated! Be Renewed! Be Inspired! Be Loving! Be Thankful! Be Happy!

215. A Person who is Believing 4 something he can't see is operating in Faith & will surely be rewarded because FAITH Pleases GOD! FAITH moves GOD not Self - Pity!

216. The Struggles of Life are 2 make us not break us! That's why in the mist of defeat I keep looking 4 Victory! Keep Hitting! Keep Trying! The Tide Always Comes Back!

217. Worries arise in the mind of man when he assumes in his mind that the cards Life has dealt him he cannot handle! GOD sends us nothing he knows we can't handle!

218. In order 2 get something new sometimes we got to get rid of something old because 2 much of the past can clutter up our Future!

219. People are paid not merely 4 what they know but more particularly 4 what they do with what they know! Make full use of the abilities GOD has give you!

220. Every Human being comes 2 Earth Custom Made Uniquely put together 4 a Specific Purpose in Life!

A Reason 4 Existence is what the Heart yearns 4! BE PURPOSEFUL!

221. Doubt is a Great hesitator hesitating at every decision along the way! Time runs out on him who Doubts 2 long! Decision Makers make Decisions that Decide Futures!

222. The more difficult the problem the Greater the Amount of Knowledge that is Ultimately Gained! May our Adversity give us Fresh Understanding & make us Better not Bitter!

223. In Life if something is 2 be Respected it 1st must be Tested! Results speak a language that mere words cannot Express! The Proof is in what we do not what we say!

224. Self Discovery is of Top Priority! Man's Ultimate Aim in Life Should be finding out who he is & What he is all about! We are all in a state of BECOMING what you BECOME is up 2 you!

225. We are all creatures of Habit clinging 2 that which satisfies the hunger of the flesh! We put down one Habit only 2 pick up another Habit because we are HABITUAL!

226. The Secret 2 getting anything done is simply 2 Act! DO IT NOW put not off 4 tomorrow what you can do 2day! Have that DO IT NOW Attitude & Watch things get done!

227. When relationships come 2 & end it is Good 2 take time 2 yourself in order that you may be completely healed! Many people are afraid 2 be alone so they rush

in2 other Unions before successfully dealing with the last one!

228. What we Trust We Love! What we don't Trust we don't Love! TRUST is what LOVE is Made of! Any relationship that is not built on TRUST will not last very long!

229. Prayer is great Mental Medicine for a tired and weary mind! I Believe in the power of PRAYER! IT WORKS! Watch things get better for you because I have been Praying for you!

230. Knowing that you can count on you shifts the Attitude from Self Defeating Thoughts to I CAN DO IT THINKING! Think the best about you! Know that you can if you Think You can!

231. The Best Remedy for depression besides Motivation from GOD above is ACTIVITY! Exercise gets the blood circulating more air to the brain makes the mind Think Better!

232. You are not the only one struggling! You're not the only one who gets depressed! You're not the only one with faults! You're not the only one Praying! Like Michael Jackson sung You're not alone!

233. Our need is GOD'S chance to show up in our lives and help us through the tough times! Seize the Opportunity call on GOD for help so the power of GOD CAN REST ON YOU!

234. We live in a world where no to things are the same but yet the world tends to condemn the man who chooses

to be different! Your fingerprint says there's only one you!

235. My dad died without teaching me anything or doing absolutely anything for me! I'm not angry it just pushed me to be a better dad than he was! May we be better parents than our parents!

236. We are what we feed ourselves! If we feed our mind negative things it will be negative! If we feed our mind positive things it will be positive! EAT GOOD FEEL GOOD!

237. What we use gets stronger with each use! What we don't use gets weaker from non use! Exercise your physical and mental muscles because what we don't use we lose!

238. Giving is a blessing as giving is a blessing! Giver and receiver are equally blessed! One must know how to give and one must know how to give!

239. A new year gives us a opportunity to start over and do things differently! Doing it Bigger and better than the previous year! Be renewed with newness! Be NEW Be a Better You!

240. Some people change some people remain the same! Why not change if what you do doesn't make you happy and why change if what you do makes you happy! Happiness is the Goal!

241. Do something fun and exciting! Have a Good Time! Enjoy yourself! Laugh out Loud! Appreciate Life! Reach

for the stars! Show love to those who you know need a little love!

242. If we are weak in a world that requires us to be strong we won't last too long! The animal kingdom teaches us only the strong survive the weak get gobbles up! BE STRONG!

243. When we change what we believe we change what we do! Change is a risk it either worsens you or it betters you! It all depends on what you believe!

244. Knowing what you want out of life gets us that much closer to reaching that which we are reaching for! Knowing is half the battle using what you know is the other half!

245. I'm never going to stop believing! I'm never going to give up on GOD! Through the storm my mind assures me that GOD KNOWS what he's doing! Ain't no QUITING ! I'M IN IT 2 WIN IT!

246. If we aren't busy Living then it's True 2 say that our bodies will be busy dying! Take care of the body and the body will allows you to Live a Beautiful Life! BE ACTIVE!

247. I don't claim to be holy! I don't pretend to be without fault! I'm in no position to judge any! I'm just letting the Spirit of GOD use me is all! Don't see me See GOD!

248. When Opportunity presents you with an Opportunity to be more than what you currently are and you Feel

Good about it, Take It! Great Opportunities are missed because of fear!

249. When we as a people come together as one all systems of this world will have to be changed to accommodate our Forward Movement! Get Involved and our problems are solved!

250. The Majority of what we know and have comes from the Teachings of someone else! Be Self Taught! If they won't Teach me then I will Teach Myself!

251. Emotional issues use up a lot of tissues! Hard Times conjure up many tears in the eyes of the Hopeless but Smiles accompany him who has unwavering FAITH!

252. The quicker we are to detach ourselves from old things that have become stale and outdated the quicker we will be able to receive New and Fresh Things!

253. Doing more! Loving more! Being more! Having more! Knowing more! Giving more! Expecting more! I want more I desire more I yearn for MORE! That's what's on my mind!

254. Wrong doesn't bring lasting Happiness! Wrong doesn't bring Peace doing the right thing does! What's wrong to you might not be wrong to me and what's wrong to you might not be wrong to me!

255. When something Ends something Begins for something to Begin something must come to an End! The Beginning of Healing is the Ending of our pain! I pray for Better Days!

256. The Right Things we do should far outweigh the wrong or bad things we do! If you do more GOOD than you do bad things shouldn't Heaven be your Reward!

257. What we Love stays on the Mind without any Conscious Effort! Who we LOVE gets the Majority of our Attention and Time! How we LOVE is How we've been LOVED!

258. The hardest thing for someone to do when someone offends them is to hold their tongue! He who holds his Tongue avoids unnecessary troubles! Tame my Tongue LORD!

259. Where there is a long line of people standing something Good is being served! Business 101: If your service or product is Good you won't be able to keep them away!

260. Life seems to require that we first pay our dues by over coming many hardships and conquering the selfish side of us before we can experience the fruits of our labor!

261. I read a book that told me I could be anything I wanted to be if I was willing to put in the time and effort to make it happen!

262. Do you Believe what you read or do you only read what you Believe!

263. Everyone has their own Individual Lives to Live! No matter how hard we plead our Loved ones must walk that walk for themselves! You handle you and let GOD handle them!

264. My Life is not my Life anymore I do nothing in my own power! I found out anything that is outside GOD'S will won't work!

265. Where GOD is is where I want to Be!

266. Hey my Friend there is a Higher you a Better you materializing on the inside of you! Believing that you have the Power to Achieve gives you the power to Achieve!

267. One does not really Appreciate what one has until one loses what one has or had! Don't be in a rush to trade in your Good Thing for something that you think is a Better Thing!

268. The More Wisdom I give the more Wisdom I get! In order to get what GOD has we must unselfishly let go of what we have! What we have is because of what we gave!

269. A Good Coach Utilizes all his or her players putting each player in his or proper position thereby Maximizing their potential! On a Team everyone is Important!

270. When something is dull more strength is needed for the task but if your skills are sharp little effort will have to be made on your behalf! Struggle is a Pencil Sharpener!

271. Everyone one has their OWN OPINION! In my Opinion everyone's Opinion should be Respected! For we Know not what that person has been through for them to have an Opinion like the one they have!

272. Who knows if our Prayers reach the Ears of a GOD whom we have never had the Privilege of seeing with our physical eyes! I just KNOW it can't hurt to Pray!

273. When one is focused on what one wants nothing is able to distract him from his targeted goal! Unless one is able to focus what one looks at will remain blurry!

274. We can think our way out of any tough situation if we would just remain calm! Calmness is a Great Eraser of Problems! When things get hectic Take Time to Think!

275. Repeating the same behavior gets us the same results every time! Different results come from doing things differently! Be Blessed in Every way!

276. He who is able to understand the handwriting on the Wall has learned that he can enjoy less stress and More success in his or her life! See the signs GOD is sending your way!

277. If we hold on to our Faith long enough a door will eventually be opened up for us! It might not be the one you where thinking about but it will ultimately prove for your good!

278. GOD never requires anything more of us than what he has already built into us! The tools you have let you know what job you are to perform! You were created for a Purpose!

279. God is the Author and Finisher of our Life and Destiny! GOD wrote the story I'm just playing the role the writer

wrote for me! Are you playing the part the Creator planned for you!

280. Having a relationship with GOD does strengthen our Knowledge of his will but we never completely see all GOD is trying to do! GOD is working his Magic behind the scene!

281. Many people live their lives trying to please other people instead of living a life that is pleasing to them! Some treat others better than they treat themselves!

282. I just don't want to know who GOD is I want GOD to know who I am! I just don't want to talk to GOD I want GOD to talk to me! I just don't want to go to Heaven I want Heaven on Earth!

283. BIG THINKER make BIG THINGS Happen small thinkers barely make small things happen! My Thinking has become too BIG for that little box they had me in!

284. Our kid's report card is a reflection of our parenting skills showing if we are involved or not! When I see the child I see the parent! Everything starts at home!

285. I'm just trying to be the best human and spiritual being that I can be! GOD is the BOSS so forgive me for trying to impress MY MAKER because the best promotions come from above!

286. He who applies his heart and mind to really understand will get that which he seeks! GOD denies us nothing that he knows is going to be for the good of all humanity!

287. I LOVE what WORDS CAN DO! I LOVE the HOPE that WORDS give! I LOVE the Power of Powerful WORDS! I LOVE WORDS because WORDS are Spirit and WORDS are Life! Yes I BELIEVE WORDS HEAL!

288. I can see the Finish Line! I can see the sea shore! I can see the season's changing! I've Learned to see beyond the not so Pleasant times in my life! LORD Help us to see!

289. What GOD SAID Yesterday was for Yesterday's Issues what GOD is saying today is for today's circumstances! Old ways and Old Things don't mix well with New Ways and New Things!

290. One should use one Imagination to paint the most beautiful picture in his mind about his future! What the mind conceives it tends to Believe! GO MIND POWER!

291. Some Things Change and are never again the same! We stay in relationships trying to rekindle the magic but that feeling we are looking for never comes back! O well time to move on!

292. He who is afraid to fail never goes beyond the Comfort Zone he has setup for himself! The only Thing I'm afraid of is Being Afraid! Move fear you're not wanted here!

293. Nothing is ever as bad as we Imagined it would be and nothing is ever as easy as we Thought it would be! No matter how it unfolds KNOW You have the Strength to overcome!

294. I tell you the things we have to go through in this life will make the Strongest Man in the world drop to his knees from the fatigue of trying to survive!

295. We can go from place to place looking for something better than where we are but if we take that same attitude with us all we're going to get is different place same mess!

296. When you don't know what to do PRAY! When you're sick in your body PRAY! When you're bored with nothing to do PRAY! When you're sad or angry PRAY! PRAY and Praise GOD IF ALL IS GOOD!

297. The best change is gradual change the type of change that has us changing without us even knowing we have been changed! Quick change shocks gradual change calms!

298. Unproductive relationships produce nothing! We waste Precious Energy trying to make work that which is not meant to work! Or you can try and try and try until you can't try any more!

299. Greener pastures awaits the bold and fearless!

300. What Qualifies a Leader to be a Leader is he wasn't afraid to Take the Lead! Be not afraid to step into the unknown!

301. In the beginning of any union one must make it clearly understood what is expected of each! To avoid misunderstandings make sure everybody is on the same page!

302. We think we have seen heard or had the best until something or someone better comes along! GOD'S BEST is yet to be unleashed! I'm Expecting Great Things from our CREATOR!

303. When something is Truly for you nothing and no one can stop you from taking possession of that which is rightfully yours! You're Blessed to have the OWNER of the World on your side!

304. Even though you didn't sneeze I'm going to say BLESS YOU! Even though you didn't ask me to I'm going to pray for you! Even though you thought no one cared I'm here to say KEEP YOUR HEAD UP and I CARE!

305. GOD Sees through me! GOD Hears through me! GOD Writes and Speaks through me! GOD Motivates and Inspires through me! But Most of All GOD LOVES THROUGH ME!

306. He who doesn't know himself doesn't no very much! In order 2 conquer the world out there You got 2 Conquer the man in here! Self knowledge is the Starting Place!

307. Weather you Believe in GOD or not you're going 2 go through your share of Test and Trials! The things we Experience make us Who we are! How we deal with it makes us What we are!

308. All one has 2 do 2 Achieve his Goals in Life is 2 just Keep putting forth a Great Effort! We have everything 2 Gain and nothing 2 lose by simply trying!

309. Anything in Life that is Worth having is Worth working for! What we work hard for we Appreciate more!

310. If Success was easy everybody would be Successful! Keep Striving!

311. Learning 2 Express yourself 2 others Frees you up! It lightens the load because you're not carrying that burden around in your heart anymore! What you been through is going 2 help someone else!

312. Struggle is only intended 2 get us 2 the place where we are Suppose 2 be in Life! An overwhelming Sense of Peace comes over you when you are where you are truly Supposed 2 be!

313. When Opportunity presents you with and Opportunity 2 be more than what you currently are and you feel good about it, Take it! Great Opportunities are missed because of fear!

314. When we as a people come together as one All systems of this world will have 2 be changed 2 accommodate our Forward Movement! Get Involved and our problems are Solved!

315. Never give up! Never throw in the towel! Never lose Hope! Never Accept Defeat! Never Quit Trying! Whatever you do Never Lose Faith in GOD because GOD Truly LOVES YOU!

316. Dumb people do dumb things because they are dumb! It should be a crime 2 be dumb because dumb

people commit most of the crimes! Do you see why EDUCATION IS SO IMPORTANT!

317. When life is at it's hardest having a reason 2 live is all you need 2 keep on living! You were Created by GOD for a PURPOSE so Live and not Die!

318. Why do 2 others what you wouldn't won't done 2 yourself! If you can't take it don't dish it out because in one form or another it's coming back! Be Good Don't hurt nobody!

319. I'm just getting what I EXPECT! I EXPECT 2 have a Great Day! I EXPECT 2 be Healthy and Wealthy! I EXPECT GOD 2 give me the Right Messages 2 Relay 2 you! I EXPECT 2 GET BETTA BAA'BBIE!

320. Don't preach 2 me about the wrong that I do if you're not going 2 preach about the wrong that you do! If you're without fault or wrong then GOD is a lie and GOD don't lie!

321. Are you Truly ready for that which you have been long waiting for! In your Getting ready for that which you seek know that Preparation and Practice Breeds Confidence!

322. People shouldn't Expect more out of you than you expect out of yourself! If anybody Raises the Bar it should be the one trying 2 jump over the bar! How high is your bar!

323. It makes the Spirit feel good 2 Learn something new 2 know something it didn't know yesterday! If you don't Educate your Spirit it won't know the Power it has!

324. It's a sad thing but some people will never change they are just too stuck in their ways! Why does something drastic have 2 happen to us before our eyes can finally be opened!

325. Some people are easy to Love and some people are hard to Love but in the end everyone needs a little Love! Love first because LOVE is the Answer and LOVE is the Solution!

326. Find something to laugh about! Think about something that made you laugh in the past and begin to laugh about it! I Wish for you to laugh because Laughter is Great Medicine!

327. If I hadn't gone through my share of pain and suffering I wouldn't have had much to talk or write about! To get through you got to Go Through! GOD wrote a Good Ending to my story!

328. I've been through too much to give up now! I come too far with GOD to turn back now! I can't give up on my Dreams now because if I do all my PAIN would have been for nothing!

329. You Know when you got company coming over you straighten up and clean up the house! In that same way Be forever Ready my friend because you never know when GOD'S COMING!

330. If we could feel the pain we cause someone else I don't think there would be much pain in the world! He who hurts another is sowing seeds to hurt his future self!

331. Happiness gives you energy! Purpose gives you energy! Hope gives you energy! Love gives you energy! Energetic people give you energy! May GOD Increase your energy!

332. We don't know what we can do without until we are forced to do without that which we thought we couldn't do without! You can do it! You just don't know you can do it!

333. We shouldn't ask for Success and then plan for Failure!

334. If you BELIEVE in you what difference does it make if those haters doubt your abilities! BELIEVE IN YOU my friend!

335. He who cannot carry his own weight will have to be carried by someone else who is able to carry both loads!

336. He who is unprepared becomes a burden to him who is prepared!

337. Everybody's looking for Love but hardly anybody's looking to Love!

338. Until one is able to Love him or herself Loving someone else is Virtually Impossible!

339. Wisdom told me, How you can Expect something to happen for you if you don't Get Out and do something to make something happen for you!

340. Dreams aren't reached by just Dreaming about them!

341. If I weren't Believing in my heart that things were going to GET BETTA I tell you, I wouldn't want to remain in this world! I HAVE FAITH IN BETTER DAYS so I'm Here to Stay!

342. Victory is Mine! Victory is Mine! Today Victory is Mine! I'm just claiming the Victory because I ALREADY WON!

343. Be it unto me according to the way I mostly think!

344. What have you learned about you! What have you learned about the people and things around you!

345. What have you learned from this earthly Experience! GOD'S Concern is that we LEARN!

346. He who lives should live to GET BETTA! He should be about Improving on his weaknesses and Getting Stronger on his Strengths! Ain't nothing wrong with GETN BETTA!

347. Lonely feelings never go away when you're alone! Human Contact is Good for the isolated spirit so GOD gave Adam Eve OOPS that's when everything went wrong!

348. If you can't see that means either you're blind or in the dark! If you can't hear that means you're either deaf or

got too much wax in your ear! If you can See and Hear BLESSED ARE YOU!

349. Your Purpose is an easy task for you to perform because it's what you were created or birthed into this world to do! When you find your Purpose then you done found everything!

350. You can't Trust what lies to you! Trust is what makes you Love a person so much! If it ain't built on Trust then it's not built on anything! Who can and do you TRUST!

351. You can never be totally sure of the thing or person you place your Confidence in! You just got to Hope that what you Trust is worth the risk of Trusting! TRUST IS A RISK!

352. Every action we take we should ask ourselves IS IT WORTH IT! If I do this IS IT WORTH IT! If I go there IS IT WORTH IT! Weigh your options IS IT WORTH IT!

353. Its more tiring doing nothing than doing something! Get your rest then get moving because too much rest wearies the body! You don't get energy by standing still but by moving around!

354. GOOD NEWS take away my Blues If I done paid my dues because GOOD NEWS is what my heart can use! It's a Blessing to be the Bringer of GOOD NEWS! GOD LOVES YOU!

355. Be All you can be! Push yourself to the Limit! Try something you never tried before! Go somewhere you

never gone before! Do the Impossible! Dream Big Dreams! Reach for the Stars!

356. You're Loved if you didn't know! You're Awesome if you didn't know! You're Strong Spirited if you didn't know! You're Very Special 2 GOD if you didn't know! IF YOU DIDN'T KNOW NOW YOU KNOW!

357. I'm not blind 2 the harsh realities of Life! I just choose 2 Focus on the Beautiful Things Life has 2 Offer! We See what we want 2 See and Hear what we want 2 Hear!

358. GOD made me 2 Love through me! GOD made me 2 Write through me! GOD made me 2 Create through me! I didn't make me GOD MADE ME! I was made 2 Get this Crazy World right!

359. We are all sometimes stuck in the middle of what we want 2 do and what we need 2 do! I was just Hoping and Praying that what I want is what GOD wants for my Life!

360. Life gives the man More who uses Well that which he already Has! You have been Faithful over a little so now I will make you Ruler over A lot, says the Good Lord!

361. It's ok 2 hear something Good but do you put 2 Practice what you Hear! 2 be a Hearer only of the Word does us no Good but 2 be a Doer of what we hear is Priceless!

362. 2 be Holy is not the absents of sin but the presence of Generosity Toward Humanity! Purity is Best Demonstrated thorough our Acts of Sharing and our Acts of Love!

363. Where do you run when you have no where 2 run! We've been running since the Slavery days! When you can't run no more You Stop You Stand and You Fight if necessary!

364. Nothing just Ups and Fixes itself! If its Broke you're going 2 need someone who Knows what they're doing 2 FIX IT! This world is so Broke and Messed Up Only GOD CAN FIX IT!

365. If you ever had a toothache you know it throws your whole body out of whack! We human beings are one body so if one hurts We all hurt! The pain you Feel is the Pain I feel!

366. When Communication Breaks down Relationships Break Down! No Communication No Relationship! Talking it out Getting it out in the Air Solves A lot of Problems!

Biography

My name is Jimmy Lee Robinson; I was born August 5 1973 in the town of Pine Bluff Arkansas. I have three beautiful children Jimia, Styles, and Zaniah. I have one older sister (Jackie) and two younger brothers Larry and Rodney and we lost one sister (Connie) to cancer at a very young age. My lovely mothers name is Beverly (Diane). I received my high school Diploma from Dollarway High school in 1992 and played on two state championship football teams and we also held the nation's longest winning streak at 51 games. In 1998 I graduated from the University of Arkansas at Pine Bluff (Historically Black College) with a Bachelors Degree in Parks and Community Recreation. I also played for the Golden Lions football team. I was a Captain and a three-year starter at defensive cornerback. I spent my summer vacation as a lifeguard at the local swimming pool, where I taught swimming classes to the children in the community. I also coached my own baseball and tee-ball team in which my daughter and son starred on. I am a mentor and tutor in the local school districts and class helper at my daughter's school.

I have held several managerial positions in corporate America and loved being a substitute teacher in local school districts. I have visited many different states since graduating from college looking for that right opportunity and that perfect fit, which has led me to venture out on my own doing what I love to do the most, writing and talking about the Goodness and Glory of GOD. I stepped out on Faith and Faith alone.

When it comes to my walk with GOD I've been walking hard and serious with GOD for about seven years now, a journey that will never end. My first Love and allegiance is to GOD who sent his Son Jesus Christ to Save the World. I like all kinds of music. I love to write and perform poetry, do motivational rap, and dance and make people laugh. I like to serve. I have performed at a lot of schools, churches and community organizations over the years. I believe I'm here to uplift GOD by uplifting his creations. To sum up what I'm all about in one word is LOVE. I speak Love, I breathe Love, and I bleed Love it is the foundation on which I stand. My desire is to be the very essence of what Love is and what GOD is all about. I'm about Love and Unity nothing else. Teamwork can't be beat! I believe Life is about human development so I'm just developing myself! My favorite Motto is GET BETTA BAA'BBIE! I believe there's no limit to what we can do when we come together! My Ultimate mission in life is to UNITE the World!